WHAT YOUR COLLEAGUES ARE SAYING . . .

"How many times have you heard 'a picture is worth a thousand words'? Visual, graphic information is important because human brains are hard-wired to attend to images. The challenge is that students still have to read words to achieve success. In this text, Lapp, Wolsey, and Wood make a vital connection between reading words and the role of graphics. They demonstrate how teachers and students can blend the two such that great learning occurs in every classroom, every day."

—DOUGLAS FISHER

Coauthor of *Rigorous Reading*

"Lapp, Wolsey, and Wood have written a book that will become *the* resource for using graphic organizers across disciplines! With careful attention to the details teachers crave in order to design meaningful lessons, the authors guide teachers on a journey that takes them far beyond the traditional uses of graphic organizers—jotting notes and organizing information—and show teachers how these visual tools lead students to independent thinking and inquiry, as well as support the Common Core reading and writing standards. What I love about this book is that it fosters original thinking among students as they design graphic organizers that enable them to unpack meaning from complex texts and develop arguments for essays."

—LAURA ROBB

Author of *Vocabulary Is Comprehension*

"Professional books have long urged teachers to use graphic organizers, but most of these books are dreadfully short on specifics. Diane Lapp and her colleagues have addressed this problem in an admirable fashion. They examine with care the kinds of organizers available to teachers, together with when and how to use them. And by showing how organizers transcend disciplinary boundaries, the authors pave the way for a school-wide focus for professional learning. Educators endeavoring to meet the challenges of the Common Core should mark this title as a must-read. This engaging book is long overdue and I recommend it enthusiastically!"

—MICHAEL MCKENNA

Coauthor of *Assessment for Reading Instruction,* Second Edition

"For educators looking for ways to implement graphic organizers in their classrooms, this is the resource for you. The numerous types of graphic organizers, the research behind them, and the how and why to use them with students are all at your fingertips. I envision this book being especially helpful for teachers new to the field just learning about graphic organizers."

—LESLIE BLAUMAN

Author of *The Common Core Companion, Grades 3–5*

MINING

COMPLEX TEXT

GRADES
2–5

We are fortunate to work with so many exemplary teachers of elementary students,
and we learn so much from them every time we visit their classrooms.
This book is dedicated to the teachers it has been our privilege to know.

GRADES
2–5

MINING
COMPLEX TEXT

Using and Creating **GRAPHIC ORGANIZERS** to Grasp Content and Share New Understandings

Diane Lapp
Thomas DeVere Wolsey
Karen Wood

CL CORWIN
LITERACY

FOR INFORMATION:

Corwin

A SAGE Company

2455 Teller Road

Thousand Oaks, California 91320

(800) 233–9936

www.corwin.com

SAGE Publications Ltd.

1 Oliver's Yard

55 City Road

London EC1Y 1SP

United Kingdom

SAGE Publications India Pvt. Ltd.

B 1/I 1 Mohan Cooperative Industrial Area

Mathura Road, New Delhi 110 044

India

SAGE Publications Asia-Pacific Pte. Ltd.

3 Church Street

#10–04 Samsung Hub

Singapore 049483

Publisher: Lisa Luedeke

Development Editor: Wendy Murray

Editorial Development Manager: Julie Nemer

Editorial Assistant: Emeli Warren

Production Editors: Olivia Weber-Stenis and Melanie Birdsall

Copy Editor: Sarah J. Duffy

Typesetter: C&M Digitals (P) Ltd.

Proofreader: Laura Webb

Indexer: Sylvia Coates

Cover and Interior Designer: Scott Van Atta

Marketing Manager: Maura Sullivan

Printed in the United States of America

A catalog record of this book is available from the Library of Congress.

ISBN: 978-1-4833-1629-1

This book is printed on acid-free paper.

Certified Chain of Custody
Promoting Sustainable Forestry
www.sfiprogram.org
SFI-01268

SFI label applies to text stock

14 15 16 17 18 10 9 8 7 6 5 4 3 2 1

CONTENTS

Acknowledgments   **xi**

CHAPTER 1   **Graphic Organizers: Making
                the Complex Comprehensible**   **1**

▶ How to Think About Standards Alignment   2
▶ How to Help Students Meet the Standards   3
▶ Tips for Using Graphic Organizers Dynamically   7
▶ How to Meet Eight Intertwined Academic Goals   8
      1. Acquire and use academic language appropriately   8
      2. Make connections   9
      3. Comprehend complex processes or events   9
      4. Understand five types of informational text structures   9
      5. Understand content   10
      6. Explore a concept and determine the nature of inquiry   10
      7. Synthesize multiple sources   10
      8. Use reliable sources to form and write opinions   11
▶ What Lies Ahead in This Book   11

CHAPTER 2   **Thinking on the Page: The Research
                Behind Why Graphic Organizers Work**   **15**

▶ Picture This: Visuals Quicken and Deepen Text Learning   17
▶ General Tips: How to Use Graphic Organizers Well   18
▶ Tiered Organizers: Scaffold Student Progress   22
▶ Examples of Tiered Graphic Organizers   24
▶ Adapting Graphic Organizers for Tiered Learning   26
▶ A Sample Tiered Lesson   27
▶ At-a-Glance Chart of Graphic Organizers Matched to Academic Goals   31

CHAPTER 3   **Using Graphic Organizers to
                Acquire Academic Vocabulary**   **33**

▶ Frayer Organizer   34
▶ Concept/Definition Map   39
▶ Word Map   43

**CHAPTER 4   Graphic Organizers Support Literary
Text Reading and Writing Tasks**   **47**

▶   Character Graphic   34
▶   Freytag's Pyramid   53

**CHAPTER 5   Graphic Organizers Support Informational
Text Reading and Writing Tasks**   **57**

▶   Text Search and Find Board   58
▶   4-Square With a Diamond   62
▶   Modified KWL   65
▶   Tabbed Book Manipulative   70

**CHAPTER 6   Graphic Organizers Support
Students' Reading Proficiencies**   **73**

▶   Somebody-Wanted-But-So   74
▶   Understanding Text Structures: Five Text Types   78
   •   Sequential   80
   •   Descriptive   81
   •   Cause/Effect   82
   •   Compare and Contrast   83
   •   Problem/Solution   85

**CHAPTER 7   Graphic Organizers Boost
Questioning and Responding**   **91**

▶   I-Chart and I-Guide   92
▶   Flip Chart Manipulative   97
▶   Text-Dependent Question/Response Organizer   99

**CHAPTER 8   Graphic Organizers Foster Reading,
Forming, and Writing Opinions**   **105**

▶   Six-Part Opinion Organizer   108
▶   Thinking Map   111

CHAPTER 9   Graphic Organizers Support Collaboration **115**

▶   Project Management Organizer   116

Conclusion   **123**

Appendix   **125**

▶   Graphic Organizers at a Glance: Meeting Eight Essential Academic Skills   125
▶   Frayer Organizer   128
▶   Concept/Definition Map   129
▶   Word Map   130
▶   Character Graphic   131
▶   Character Graphic for Younger Students   132

▶ Character Graphic for Upper Elementary Students   133

▶ Freytag's Pyramid   134

▶ Text Search and Find Board   135

▶ 4-Square With a Diamond   136

▶ KWL   137

▶ Somebody-Wanted-But-So   138

▶ Five Text Types:

   • Sequential   139

   • Descriptive   140

   • Cause/Effect   141

   • Compare and Contrast   142

   • Problem/Solution   143

▶ Compare-and-Contrast Attribute Chart   144

▶ Problem/Solution Graphic Organizer   145

▶ I-Chart   146

▶ I-Guide   147

▶ Text-Dependent Question/Response Organizer   148

▶ Six-Part Opinion Organizer   149

▶ Thinking Map   150

Glossary   **151**

References   **153**

Index   **157**

Visit the companion website at
www.corwin.com/miningcomplextext/2-5
for downloadable resources.

ACKNOWLEDGMENTS

A special thanks to teacher consultants/lesson designers extraordinaire:

Doctoral students in curriculum and instruction at the University of North Carolina–Charlotte:

Joyce Farrow, UNCC and Mooresville Graded School District, NC
Rebecca Kavel, UNCC and Charlotte Mecklenburg Schools, NC
Kyle Kester, UNCC and Davie County Schools, NC
Kim Heintschel Ramadan, UNCC and Charlotte Mecklenburg Schools, NC
Brian Williams, UNCC

Master's in reading education students at the University of North Carolina–Charlotte:

Jennifer Harahus, Cabarrus County Schools, NC
Lindsay Merritt, Hope Academy, Concord, NC

and Stacy Miller, rock star teacher at Patch American High School, Stuttgart, Germany

GRAPHIC ORGANIZERS
MAKING THE COMPLEX COMPREHENSIBLE

Graphic organizers, mind maps, knowledge maps, concept maps. Whatever you call them, chances are you've used them or created them to support students' learning. They are a powerful tool for visually representing one's understanding of information and concepts. This makes them terrific tools for assessment also, because they clearly show what students grasp—and what they don't yet fully understand.

Yet in the midst of momentum for increased depth and rigor in instruction and higher expectations of what students must be able to do in regard to complex text reading, writing, and thinking, do graphic organizers still have a role? How can a single-page tool, made up of simple shapes and a mere sprinkling of words, possibly take students where they need to go?

In this book we answer these questions by addressing why and how graphic organizers have more relevance than ever before in supporting elementary students' understanding of challenging content. We discuss why students need these tools to deeply comprehend complex ideas and present them. We explain how these visual displays help students analyze a topic or idea by separating the constituent parts or elements. These visuals allow students to look closely at the key parts of a fairy tale, the chief trade artifacts of early Americans, the rain cycle—virtually any body of information, to analyze how the parts fit together. We explore the ways graphic organizers also help students support their thinking as they work to absorb content, giving them a vehicle for writing down and arranging their understandings, which they can then share with others.

We also explore how graphic organizers serve as weigh stations on the road to extended writing, further reading, and discussion. We have worked with teachers throughout North America, and we bring to this book their depth insights regarding how to engage students in using and creating their own graphic organizers. In our research and observations in classrooms, we find teachers use graphic organizers most often to

- support students' comprehension of a text;
- promote students' oral sharing of information and their ideas;
- elevate organized note-taking while listening to information and, as our colleagues Fisher and Frey (2012a) suggest, note-making while interacting with complex texts;
- scaffold students' narrative and informational writing throughout the process;
- move students to independent thinking as they learn to create their own organizing, note-taking, and note-making systems.

Two consistent findings from our classroom observations are that teachers wonder how to help students understand why they have to construct or complete a graphic organizer, and how they can better support students to independently craft graphic organizers that fit their individual learning purposes. Students often don't appreciate the connections between a graphic organizer and their thinking and learning. Once this link is made, they realize the power of graphic organizers for organized note-taking, note-making, and presenting information. To support you in making this information apparent to your students, the lessons and strategies throughout this book include classroom examples from teachers that demonstrate the following:

- planning sufficient classroom time to allow students to complete or develop a graphic organizer
- modeling the process for using visual tools to support thinking, inquiry, and thorough understanding of information
- sharing the intended purpose and outcome for using the graphic organizer
- engaging students in whole-class, small-group, partner, individual, and independent work using and crafting organizers
- checking, assessing, and evaluating students' work for clues to identify their understandings, confusions, and next steps

HOW TO THINK ABOUT STANDARDS ALIGNMENT

In the next section we address the Common Core State Standards, and throughout this book, you'll find specific Common Core standards referenced, so in that sense our lesson ideas are completely aligned. However, we are well aware that just about any professional resource published after 2012 is going to tout these alignments, and we feel that the specific standards kind of "grey out" if all we do is show the literal match-up and stay at a micro-level. Thus, before we discuss the academic goals in the next section, let's consider how graphic organizers help students learn the ways of thinking addressed by the Common Core State Standards or other state standards.

These four considerations are meant to help you both use the lesson scenarios in this book and generate your own lessons that will meet the Common Core's call for depth, collaboration, and students' independent application of understandings. For each organizer, we help you consider the following:

1. **why** a particular graphic organizer works well to support content learning
2. **when** to use various graphic organizers to support various learning situations
3. **how** to deliver dynamic demonstration lessons that will teach students to select and use graphic organizers independently
4. **what** to tune in to when assessing students' work in order to pinpoint strengths and needs and then plan subsequent instruction that deepens their thinking, writing, reading, and speaking

HOW TO HELP STUDENTS MEET THE STANDARDS

The Common Core consists of 32 anchor standards that are grouped into four sections that address the literacy processes of reading, writing, speaking and listening, and language behaviors. Of these English language arts (ELA) standards, at least 18 can be achieved with the support of various graphic organizers. Let's look at each of these four ELA sections, and then we'll think about them in an integrated fashion.

To begin let's consider reading anchor standards 1 and 10 of the Common Core State Standards (CCSS; Common Core State Standards Initiative, 2010b).

CCSS.R.1.

Read closely to determine what the text says and to make logical inferences from it; cite specific textual information when writing or speaking to support conclusions drawn from the text.

CCSS.R.10.

Read and comprehend complex literary and informational texts independently and proficiently.

Notice that these two standards state that students are expected to be able to read increasingly complex texts. Doing so involves a host of thinking processes, including analyzing, comparing, and evaluating. Graphic organizers support each of these processes.

Now let's consider the 16 other ELA anchor standards for which we think graphic organizers are particularly well suited. As you read each standard, see if you agree with the type of graphic we would craft; there is no one right answer. We pose some questions to get you thinking about custom creating your own.

Selected Common Core **Reading** Anchor Standards Calling for Graphic Organizers

CCRA.R.3.

Analyze how and why individuals, events, and ideas develop and interact over the course of a text.

A graphic organizer would allow students to add information to it throughout the reading. Can you envision how its design would support students noticing the interactions and evolution of people, events, concepts?

CCRA.R.5.

Analyze the structure of texts, including how specific sentences, paragraphs, and larger portions of the text (e.g., a section, chapter, scene, or stanza) relate to each other and the whole.

Do you agree that this standard calls for a visual that supports the reader in seeing the parts of the whole?

CCRA.R.7.

Integrate and evaluate content presented in diverse media and formats, including visually and quantitatively, as well as in words.

Are you seeing a chart graphic being used here?

CCRA.R.8.

Delineate and evaluate the argument and specific claims in a text, including the validity of the reasoning as well as the relevance and sufficiency of the evidence.

Here again, this could be a graphic that helps learners establish, develop, and support an argument. Given that evaluating texts is a sophisticated skill elementary students find difficult, how might you devise the organizer to be developmentally appropriate for your students?

CCRA.R.9.

Analyze how two or more texts address similar themes or topics in order to build knowledge or to compare the approaches the authors take.

Yes, this graphic organizer might be a compare-contrast diagram. How might you use language and graphics to help your students consider both similarities and differences?

If you teach students in the intermediate grades, we encourage you to communicate to them that they don't have to wait for you to hand them a graphic organizer—they can create one on their own. Over time, students get more adept at knowing which type of organizer might help them best display their thinking.

Selected Common Core **Writing** Anchor Standards Calling for Graphic Organizers

When we turn to the anchor standards for writing, it's easy to envision how graphic organizers support all the behaviors involved in composing work in various genres across the curriculum. Whether writing an opinion piece, a book review, or a literary work, organizers support elementary students as they develop their ability to sequence and organize their details/text evidence and line of thought. Once again, we share our thinking about the graphics we might select or create in order to accomplish the tasks identified in each standard.

CCRA.W.4.

Produce clear and coherent writing in which the development, organization, and style are appropriate to task, purpose, and audience.

Graphic organizers that include structure and scaffolding shapes would help students organize sentences and paragraphs. How would you prompt students to consider task, purpose, and audience as they complete the organizer?

CCRA.W.7.

Conduct short as well as more sustained research projects based on focused questions, demonstrating understanding of the subject under investigation.

Because this standard calls for students to focus their research, it would be ideal to craft graphic organizers that include questions to help students tightly frame their research so that it's manageable. How might you design the organizer so that it also helps students organize their ideas as they write about the content? Would including writing prompts help guide them to fully demonstrate their knowledge?

CCRA.W.8.

Gather relevant information from multiple print and digital sources, assess the credibility and accuracy of each source, and integrate the information while avoiding plagiarism.

This would call for a graphic that invites a comparison of information across texts. How might you tailor this—any organizer—to the age and stage of the students you teach?

CCRA.W.9.

Draw evidence from literary or informational texts to support analysis, reflection, and research.

This organizer would nudge students to go back in to the text to support their responses, so it would need to include areas that represent initial information and growing reflections. How might you set it up to remind young learners of the types of evidence to use (e.g., key facts, character quotes, dates)?

Selected Common Core **Speaking and Listening** Anchor Standards Calling for Graphic Organizers

Being able to organize information to share orally is central to the speaking and listening standards. Again we invite you to think about the dimensions of a graphic organizer that would support students as they organize information and understandings and share them with others.

CCRA.SL.2.

Integrate and evaluate information presented in diverse media and formats, including visually, quantitatively, and orally.

This graphic would need to support students' analysis across text types. How might you prompt students to both select information and evaluate it?

CCRA.SL.4.

Present information, findings, and supporting evidence such that listeners can follow the line of reasoning and the organization, development, and style are appropriate to task, purpose, and audience.

This graphic might be a chart showing how a complex idea is developed over time. Might you also include a checklist that helps students effectively present information?

CCRA.SL.5.

Make strategic use of digital media and visual displays of data to express information and enhance understanding of presentations.

Illustrating information through multiple mediums will certainly promote comprehension of the information. Is there an existing graphic that does this, or will you need to redesign an existing one or create a new design to accomplish this?

A variety of graphic organizers shared in this text support organizing one's ideas and information through formats that are comprehensible. Many can accomplish these identified ELA anchor standards, which of course are addressed across the grade levels through ascending or increasing levels of complexity. We urge you to teach your students to not stop with just the organizers we have shared. Their independence results from thinking on their own about the information they are attempting to organize or share and then crafting a graphic that helps them do so. Invite them to use ours as models for their own creations. Once they understand why they are using graphic organizers, encourage them to take the lead in selection or design. Their selections or creations will provide you with rich insights about their thinking.

Selected Common Core **Language** Anchor Standards Calling for Graphic Organizers

In the following language anchor standards, notice that here, again, there is an emphasis on students collaborating with peers and communicating with others. Graphic organizers lend themselves to partner and small-group work, and we encourage you to think about a variety of ways students can contribute. For example, students might be responsible for completing particular sections; each student might complete one and then bring it to a small group to compile ideas into a final version. Students can assume roles as text researchers, writers, presenters, and so on.

CCRA.L.1.

Prepare for and participate effectively in a range of conversations and collaborations with diverse partners, building on others' ideas and expressing their own clearly and persuasively.

This graphic would need to involve the space for a student to collect his or her own ideas and also a section that invites comparison. How might you encourage collaboration? How might you ensure diverse partners and good quality of conversation?

CCRA.L.2.

Integrate and evaluate information presented in diverse media and formats, including visually, quantitatively, and orally.

Students share information through multiple media. How might these be displayed? Would there need to be space for graphs, photos, and data?

Present information, findings, and supporting evidence such that listeners can follow the line of reasoning and the organization, development, and style are appropriate to task, purpose, and audience.

This standard calls for a graphic that illustrates the organizational development of an idea or thesis. How might the information best be displayed for the intended audience? And might you develop an organizer to be used by those listening to the presentation?

Make strategic use of digital media and visual displays of data to express information and enhance understanding of presentations.

Creativity should be the subtitle for this standard since it invites one to resourcefully share information through a graphic supporting multiple media. How might graphic organizers support students' creativity as they prepare to share ideas across the disciplines?

TIPS FOR USING GRAPHIC ORGANIZERS DYNAMICALLY

We are excited that so many of the ELA anchor standards immediately invite ingenious presentations of information that push beyond traditional ways of tracking, showing, and sharing student learning. A first point we want to make is that for graphic organizers to significantly contribute to student learning they have to become an essential element of learning. Students need to be engaged in selecting and devising them. Conversations about them need to occur before, during, and after learning. Without that commitment, graphic organizers weaken in their effect, becoming something to photocopy, something students dutifully complete and turn in—but not something that has truly helped them deepen pathways of thinking and creating.

Here are a few points to consider as you present a lesson involving a graphic organizer that will help you use it dynamically:

- As much as possible, invite students to help you select or create a graphic organizer. When students are involved in thinking about the *why* behind a particular organizer as it relates to curricular content or a task, it builds that critical metacognitive awareness—they're learning how to learn. One of the best gifts we can give our students is the awareness that although reams of information abound at the click of a mouse, it's each person's job to fully comprehend the *intent* of the information he or she is reading, discussing, or writing about.

- Think out loud as you select an organizer so students have a "script" of your decision making. Encourage students to join you in first identifying the purpose of the information they want to organize or share. For example, if the graphic is to support note-taking while reading a selected text, teach them to preview the text to determine the structure (story, cause/effect, etc.) the author used and then look together for an organizer that seems a good fit. If one doesn't exist, support students in creating it.

• When you want students to ultimately share information in an oral presentation or written piece, lay the groundwork at the outset of the lesson. For example, discuss and help them name their audience and purpose. Then help them determine or design a graphic organizer design that suits their purposes, their audience, and their vision for how the information is best displayed.

HOW TO MEET EIGHT INTERTWINED ACADEMIC GOALS

A second point we want to make is that even though we have just shown the potential for graphic organizers to address individual standards, in the day-to-day of the classroom, you'll be naturally bundling several standards. Reading, talking, writing, thinking, and presenting information are interwoven. So as you use the graphic organizers found in this book, remember they are designed to address several ELA standards at once.

Now, let's consider why it's important to group standards in a lesson. Think about it: When teaching we seldom address one isolated literacy practice in a lesson. As you'll see in each example shared, we suggest bundling standards to address the many literacy processes students are accomplishing in each lesson as they read, speak, listen, and write. Learning across the disciplines is directly correlated to the strength of students' literacies. Graphic organizers promote the development of these literacies by helping students chunk, organize, comprehend, and share information more effectively. Figure 1-1 shows some of the organizers you will find in this book. The following eight areas or big ideas illustrate the connection between literacy learning and graphic organizers.

1. **Acquire and use academic language appropriately.** One aspect of the Common Core standards is that students can acquire and use academic language, including vocabulary, to become conversant with content. Academic language is different in many respects from

FIGURE 1-1
Collage of Some of the Graphic Organizers You Will Discover in This Book

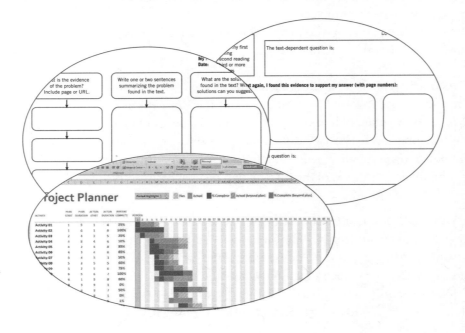

the language students (and their teachers) use in most day-to-day literacy activities, such as conversation. Academic language focuses on more specialized knowledge of academic disciplines and concepts and often requires different language registers and vocabulary (see Townsend & Lapp, 2010). Academic language features discipline-specific terms and syntactic structures as well as terms that students would not generally use in conversation, such as *abandon* or *clarify,* that cut across disciplines.

How graphic organizers help: Organizers help students visually map their thinking about content onto a single, focused page, and both the written directions and the spheres themselves have academic language embedded. Think of the popular Venn diagram: two interlocked circles and directions that ask students to *compare and contrast* something using terms that are new or used in a new way. As they create and use these organizers and the information they contain, students have opportunities to use and grow their academic language proficiencies.

2. Make connections. In some ways, making connections is the essence of learning. Neurons connect with each other to produce powerful new learning (see Zull, 2002). Readers connect what they know of how texts are coherent, how one text connects with that of another (Hartman, 1995), or how texts connect with the world as they know it (see Harvey & Goudvis, 2000).

How graphic organizers help: Organizers allow students to see, almost at a glance, how one idea relates to another or how one process is contingent upon another. Our experience tells us that students do not need to have things simplified so much as they need to see the big picture before they can look at the details. We liken this to looking at the box showing the final product of a jigsaw puzzle before spending time assembling the parts into a whole.

3. Comprehend complex processes or events (e.g., sequences). A recurring theme throughout this book is that sometimes it is necessary to make things simpler than they may first appear. Learning occurs when problems, events, concepts, and processes present a challenge to our thinking. Learning simpler constructs can lead to greater understanding of complex concepts, just as learning complex constructs might be made more comprehensible with the support of an organizing schema.

How graphic organizers help: As with other academic goals, students are frequently challenged to understand information and ideas that are complex and sometimes complicated. *Complexity* takes into account nuances and details, while *complicated* sometimes means that the steps can be confusing, in our view. Graphic organizers, in the hands of a skillful teacher, have the potential to make the complex comprehensible so that the details and nuances can be integrated into a richer understanding. They also offer the opportunity to make the complicated comprehensible as students grapple with new learning.

4. Understand five types of informational text structures. Five general, or top-level, structures of text are often found in informational material. When students know the five structures of cause/effect, problem/solution, compare and contrast, descriptive, and sequential, they have a greater chance of making the complexity of a text more comprehensible.

How graphic organizers help: Though top-level structures, such as descriptive or cause/effect, seem obvious, applying them as a reader or writer is often a challenge given the complexities of the texts students are reading and those they compose. Graphic organizers give students the visual support to discern what those top-level structures are and thereby concentrate their efforts on understanding the content.

5. **Understand content.** Students use a graphic organizer most frequently in the process of trying to learn and organize information, be it a science concept, the truth found in a work of fiction, a mathematics problem, and so on. They are trying to learn discipline-specific information.

How graphic organizers help: Graphic organizers help for a couple of reasons. The obvious reason is they help students make notes and thereby create a placeholder for facts and other information. Students develop understandings in the midst of reading and learning, making recall and analysis a bit easier. The less obvious reason is that different types of organizers work better with some students than with others and that they are tools that can be used on an as-needed basis with a select few students. In fact, when they are assigned to every student as a kind of catch-all, and when teachers' assumption is that all students' automatically understand the content and benefit from the visual organizer, results are uneven. It turns out that students seem to learn best when graphic organizers are used strategically, and as they come to know them, they can choose ones that work best for them or create ones to illustrate their thinking. It's imperative to consider the organizational patterns different students know and respond to well. There are also students who don't like to use them at all for certain purposes; those who do not need should be invited to create other ways to organize information. In many instances these become personally created graphic organizers.

6. **Explore a concept and determine the nature of inquiry.** In our experience, students learn well when they have something intriguing to investigate or a problem to be addressed. Learning is naturally a process of wondering and inquiring into many topics.

How graphic organizers help: Knowing content is one thing, but figuring out broad concepts and how those relate to an inquiry stance is quite another. Children in Grades K–6 are fabulously curious and can become content experts on rainforest life, trucks, butterfly species—you name it. But what the CCSS ask teachers to do is "flip" or apply the knowledge into interconnected investigations (e.g., How is camouflage in the rainforest connected to survival? How does preserving rainforests relate to improving human conditions in and near the rainforests?). Even students in the primary grades can engage in these bigger quests if we scaffold learning with graphic organizers, so recording, comparing, contrasting, and so on become more concrete processes.

Inquiry is often informed by the discipline involved. Scientists approach a question they have in a particular manner, writers of fiction grab us with a hook or question, and historians may choose timelines and photographs. Graphic organizers can help students understand what they need or want to know, but also how to form a framework for thinking about their inquiry even if they later propose something different than a traditional approach. Knowing *how* it has been done is often the lever (Gardner, 2006) that leads to creativity.

7. **Synthesize multiple sources.** Though students often become used to working with a single text, much learning occurs when students compare and contrast the ideas found in several sources. Synthesizing a number of sources of information while reading, during

discussion, and through composing appears to be a key skill expected in rigorous standards and in the digital age when many sources are readily available.

How graphic organizers help: Working with multiple sources of information is a key criterion for college and career readiness, but as any K–5 teacher knows, it can be a daunting task for young students. Graphic organizers provide a means of managing many diverse sources, and looking for confirming evidence for a given opinion, disconfirming evidence, and commonalities. Though teachers may choose to provide an organizer for such purposes, students are well served when they are able to recognize their own needs for an organizer and select or create one themselves. Though younger students are not always conversant enough with content and the way it is structured, teachers can help them by calling attention to the organizer and how it relates to the text they will read. As students move into higher grades, they will be better prepared to make their own choices or modify graphic organizers for specific purposes.

8. **Use reliable sources to form and write opinions.** Jumping to an opinion often short-circuits deep thinking. Everyone, it seems, has an idea about why something is the way it is, what it means, or how things should work, but effective opinions that lead to deeper understandings and conversations are based on well-considered evidence, and they are subject to refutation or disconfirming ideas. (See our companion book for older students, *Mining Complex Text, Grades 6–12*, which explores in more detail how students might use graphic organizers to scaffold and promote skills with argumentation structures and how they can become more independent at crafting their own thinking and their organizers.)

How graphic organizers help: Graphic organizers provide structures so that elementary students can more easily collect evidence, sort that evidence, and put it to use in written work or other multimodal composition tasks.

WHAT LIES AHEAD IN THIS BOOK

Throughout the book, we include marginal notes that refer to the eight academic goals or big ideas we described above; in organizing this book, we were mindful of the Common Core State Standards and related rigorous goals as well as college and career readiness outcomes. We illustrate through example how to use graphic organizers to help students engage with and comprehend timeless text types and also use and craft organizers as they think and write in genres that are evergreen as well as those that are newer, such as those found in digital environments.

Chapter 2: Thinking on the Page: The Research Behind Why Graphic Organizers Work. This chapter shares the research base illustrating how cognitive processing of information can be supported by using graphic organizers. Also noted is how graphic organizers provide learning scaffolds, quick assessment options, and the promotion of differentiated learning.

Chapter 3: Using Graphic Organizers to Acquire Academic Vocabulary. Here we demonstrate how graphic organizers can promote comprehension and use of academic language. Beginning in kindergarten students are immersed in academic language that comprises words essential to understanding content (e.g., *sink, float, community, insect,* *migration*) as well as words that describe the processes involved when reading, writing, discussing, and crafting a multimodal composition (e.g., *same, different, compare, contrast, sequence, evaluate, infer*). At the end of the book, you will find a glossary of terms that may be helpful as a reminder about the way we have used terms such as *academic language* and *academic vocabulary* throughout this book.

Chapter 4: Graphic Organizers Support Literary Text Reading and Writing Tasks. Works of fiction and informational genres of text share many qualities. However, they also differ in significant ways. This chapter shows how graphic organizers help students understand major text patterns specific to literature and help learners both read and write narrative.

Chapter 5: Graphic Organizers Support Informational Text Reading and Writing Tasks. This chapter zeroes in on how graphic organizers can extend and deepen students' thinking about expository or informational genres as both readers and writers.

Chapter 6: Graphic Organizers Support Students' Reading Proficiencies. This chapter supports teachers' objective to improve students' reading proficiency. The Common Core State Standards emphasize this goal (Common Core State Standards Initiative, 2010a). Graphic organizers that direct students' attention to specific information in a text can help them organize, analyze, summarize, and evaluate complex ideas within the "four corners" of the text (Coleman & Pimentel, 2012). In the elementary grades, special attention to top-level organizational structures and their interplay supports comprehension. As students become increasingly proficient with these and more fully understand how they work together, they also become more capable with composing tasks.

Chapter 7: Graphic Organizers Boost Questioning and Responding. No effective teacher ever said, "Gosh, I wish my students did not ask questions about what we are learning or reading!" However, students in elementary grades are not yet experts at learning as a process or with content knowledge. In this chapter we show how graphic organizers can help students know what questions to ask, how to ask them, when and where to ask those questions, and how to respond to other students and members of the community who pose questions about learning tasks and content knowledge.

Chapter 8: Graphic Organizers Foster Reading, Forming, and Writing Opinions. Opinions are a cornerstone of writing tasks for elementary students working with the Common Core and similar standards. But just what constitutes an effective and informative opinion? How might an elementary student write or otherwise express an opinion that others, who may not be of like mind, want to hear? Graphic organizers are on the job, again; they have the potential to help students think about what an opinion is and how it might persuade or convince others who do not quite think the way they do. (See our companion book for secondary teachers for more on how argumentation and graphic organizers work together from Grade 6 onward.)

Chapter 9: Graphic Organizers Support Collaboration. Most people agree that to be ready for college, career, the next grade level, or just getting a task done requires communication and collaboration. Who is going to do what? When will this occur? What class meetings did we have and what did we decide? Wait—there's a graphic organizer for that! Organizers that support collaboration are shared in this chapter.

The goal of this book is for students to learn the importance of organizing the information they are reading or presenting and, in doing so, to become confident in selecting or constructing graphic organizers to organize and share information and their ideas.

STRUCTURED OVERVIEW: GRAPHIC ORGANIZERS IN THIS BOOK

A structured overview is a type of graphic organizer that shows broad connections between and among related topics. This shows the book's content so you can see how narrower topics relate to larger concepts.

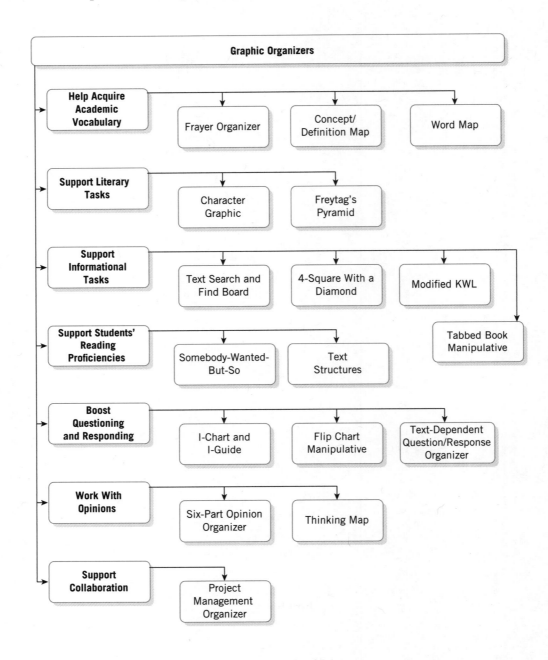

Photo by Thinkstock

THINKING ON THE PAGE

The Research Behind Why Graphic Organizers Work

We Googled "graphic organizer business" and up popped more than 14 million results! No wonder graphic organizers are popular in classrooms—they are a tool that works in the world, helping people in all sorts of fields solve some of the very same problems that students often face. For something to be that popular, it must align with how humans think, decide, and function, but more about that in a minute.

Comparing and contrasting, predicting and planning, organizing, identifying important attributes—these are just a few of the thinking processes graphic organizers help us do. To do this cognitive work, we require our brains to process information in particular ways, and in layperson's terms, this thinking not only takes up space in our brains, it plays out spatially. Neuroscience in recent years has made advances in brain imaging, and we can now see just where vocabulary and other linguistic information is stored, where spatial and visual images reside, how emotions are encoded and stimulated, and so on. Put simply, our brains are uniquely wired for two main functions: making sense of language and making sense of the visual cues that are received. In addition, scientists have made the following discoveries:

- The more connections the neurons make, the more likely it is that learning will occur and creative ideas will result.
- When brains perceive connections between visual information (say, a picture) and language, learning seems to increase.

Now think about a graphic organizer. It has both words and visuals, so it reflects both of the processing centers of our brains. In addition, a graphic organizer helps us make connections between linguistic and visual information. When our brains confront challenging topics, the layout of an organizer helps make the connections apparent to us. We can more easily spot the connection on the organizer, or our interacting with the organizer helps us arrange and spread out facts and ideas in our heads so that we are better able to have that "Aha" moment of connection.

A good way to illustrate this idea is to conduct a little experiment. Ready? Read this excerpt from an online book produced by the U.S. Army describing the U.S. Civil War battle at Gettysburg.

> As Buford had expected, Hill ordered Heth's entire division to advance on Gettysburg at first light. About 0700, troopers from the 8th Illinois Cavalry, posted three miles west of Gettysburg on the Chambersburg Pike, spotted shadowy figures nearing the Marsh Creek Bridge to their front. According to tradition, Lt. Marcellus Jones borrowed a sergeant's carbine and fired the first shot of the Battle of Gettysburg. He then fired several more rounds at skirmishers from Brig. Gen. James J. Archer's brigade, the lead element of Heth's division. Jones immediately reported the contact; in short order, Buford learned not only of the mounting threat along the Chambersburg Pike, but also of enemy activity along roads to the west and north of Gettysburg. He immediately sent brief but informative assessments to the rapidly changing situation to Mead at Army headquarters and to Maj. Gen. John F. Reynolds, whose I Corps had encamped the previous night just a few miles south of Gettysburg. (Reardon & Vossler, 2013, p. 19)

(If you would like to read the rest of the account, you can visit www.history.army.mil/html/books/075/75-10/CMH_Pub_75-10.pdf.)

Now, without looking back, can you illustrate in some way the landscape, the positions of the commanders, and just where Lieutenant Jones was when he fired the opening shot in the Battle of Gettysburg? The task is a difficult one. First, it is necessary to remember who all those people are: Heth, Hill, Buford, and so on. Then, you must know and remember for which side each commander led his troops. Also, keeping track of the abbreviations, such as "Brig. Gen." might not be so easy if you are not familiar with these sorts of accounts. As you read, you must construct in your mind some idea of the lay of the land and the sequence of events, and keep all that mentally handy as you continue to read.

If only there were some ways to make this difficult and rigorous text more comprehensible. A picture or map, perhaps, with a timeline might do it. If you could pair up the complex text you just read with some visual information—a graphic organizer—that gives you some idea of the relationships of the ideas, it just might help. Depending on what your purpose for reading is, a graphic organizer that is already constructed might be best. At other times, partially completed graphic organizers that you fill in as you read might also work. In some cases, you might want to really work with the ideas and create your own organizer. Interactive graphic organizers might include two very different visual elements: a timeline and a map.

For an example of this latter type, you can visit http://storymaps.esri.com/stories/2013/gettysburg to take a look at the interactive visual "Decisive Moments in the Battle of Gettysburg." Best of all, you can point to different places on the timeline and see which troops were moving and the direction they attempted to move. If you hover over points on the map, you will see who commanded the divisions. In some places, the timeline and map are supplemented with additional photographs and concise text. Notice how the information on the timeline is organized in sequence and linked to the information on the map—it's organized visually. By putting the interactive graphic organizer with text, the battle about which you are reading is much more comprehensible and perhaps a bit of fun, too.

PICTURE THIS: VISUALS QUICKEN AND DEEPEN TEXT LEARNING

These brains of ours are fairly amazing, and smart approaches lead to better learning. Psychologists have a theory that our brains tend to store or code information in one of two forms (Sadoski & Paivio, 2004). Information can be coded in our brains as linguistic, or language-based, knowledge, or it can be stored as imagery. Some time ago, one psychologist proposed that imagery might include physical sensations including smell and sound, among others (Richardson, 1983). For our purposes in this book, however, we generally stick with imagery in terms of visual information—a picture or chart, for example.

A term teachers often hear is *nonlinguistic representation*. Marzano, Pickering, and Pollock (2001), in their touchstone text, say that nonlinguistic representation refers to the imagery mode brains use to encode information that emphasizes that format. For example, you might encode a photograph of the battlefield at Gettysburg primarily in imagery mode because the information is presented as an image. Information you receive from reading this paragraph would be encoded primarily in the linguistic mode because language is the way the information is being conveyed. Typically, graphic organizers make use of nonlinguistic information and linguistic information from written text or spoken words; thus, the terms *nonlinguistic representation* and *graphic organizer* are related but not synonymous.

That is fairly straightforward, but there is more to it. Some generalizations from our own work in this area may help as we continue our exploration of what graphic organizers are and how they work to improve learning.

- When learners are asked to transform information in some way (say, from linguistic mode to imagery), the strength of the learning tends to increase.
- When learners are asked to pair information in imagery and linguistic mode, learning tends to increase.
- When learners are asked to create new representations, through application, analysis, evaluation, or creation (Anderson & Krathwohl, 2001), learning tends to increase.

Marzano et al. (2001) suggest that nonlinguistic representations should elaborate on knowledge. Keeping in mind the idea that graphic organizers usually blend nonlinguistic and linguistic information, we can put that notion to good use. Simply put, graphic organizers are best suited (not always, but usually) to generating knowledge or making sense of knowledge by building on the three generalizations above. How teachers construct tasks that ask for graphic organizer skills and how students learn to use and create graphic organizers is a primary focus in this book. Our goal is to help you teach your students that if a graphic organizer doesn't exist that supports their purposes, they should craft one that does. We hope that as you and your students analyze and use the ones presented in this text, they will develop the skill and craft that supports this independence.

GENERAL TIPS: HOW TO USE GRAPHIC ORGANIZERS WELL

Let's turn from the *why* to the *how*. Here are several general ideas for integrating graphic organizers into your teaching and students' learning.

Be Explicit

As with most any instructional routine or tool, students need to know how a graphic organizer operates. Without sufficient teacher modeling, young learners often assume it's a matter of simply filling in the blanks and moving on. It is very important that they know why the graphic organizer is part of their learning and how it contributes to what they might know or be able to do. As a teacher, the *why* may come from the skills embedded in a specific standard; the important thing is that you explain to your students in simple terms what it is they are being asked to do and how the organizer is going to help them. Throughout this book, we provide ideas for helping your students see the relevance of various organizers, and we often name the particular skills featured.

Use Graphic Organizers to Focus on Key Attributes and Concepts

No matter what the age, young learners have to assimilate an awful lot of new information and ideas coming at them. Graphic organizers put a frame around what kids are trying to read, trying to write, or trying to comprehend. And in a parallel manner, organizers invite teachers to chunk academic content and processes into "small frames," helping them be more intentional about the focus of their instruction, which might focus students' attention on the key steps of writing a fact book, the three essential math concepts students need to take away from the unit, or the pros and cons of an issue. In this light, the graphic organizer is an instructional planning tool. At the risk of oversimplifying, if you can envision a student's thorough understanding fitting comfortably on a single-page organizer, with just a few boxes or circles and arrows, then chances are you have a good focus on key attributes and concepts. And as we said in Chapter 1, organizers help make challenging tasks comprehensible, not just simpler (though there are times when simplifying is appropriate or as a first stage to greater understanding).

Use Graphic Organizers to
Help Students "Slice the Surface" of a Text

When what is to be learned is new, it can be a confusing array of information. That array of information may make it difficult for the novice learner, or the novice with specific content, to understand just what the key features or main ideas are. In these cases, graphic organizers can be used and revisited at each phase of a student tackling a challenging text, from skimming/previewing to after-reading reflection. To show you what we mean, here is an adult-level example:

Try this: Unless you are a particle physicist, navigate to http://home.web.cern.ch/about/physics/standard-model (see Figure 2-1), a website of the European Organization for Nuclear Research (CERN). Read the page to understand the standard model of particle physics. Click the links if you like, and read what you find there. When you are done, close your browser and come on back to this page. Go ahead—we'll wait.

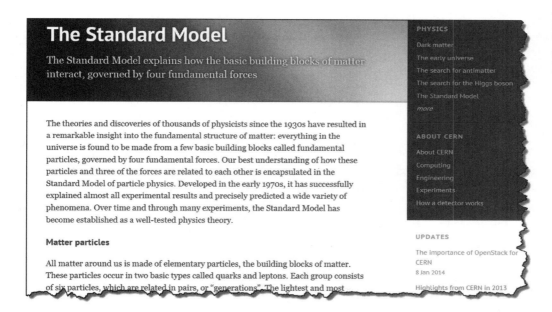

FIGURE 2-1
Web Page Describing the Standard Model of Particle Physics

Source: Screen capture is reproduced courtesy of the CERN Press Office, Geneva, Switzerland.

All done reading? Now, if you know something about particle physics, this should be a piece of cake, right? But if you are like us, particle physics is fairly complex from a conceptual standpoint and a topic about which you know very little. The web page you visited was written for a general audience, not scientists who work in this field. For those without specific prior content knowledge on which to draw, this information seems dense and overwhelming. The cognitive task is not just to simplify what is on the web page; rather, the task is to make it comprehensible. Sometimes two or three graphic organizers are needed for different purposes. Let's say that to begin understanding particle physics we think it might be a good start to visually organize the terms or vocabulary as they were encountered in the "Matter particles" paragraph. Figure 2-2 is our organizer that puts all the terms found in that paragraph in a visual order with a space for further questions. For example, we might wonder what the difference is between leptons and quarks and predict that we will learn more about that as we read.

FIGURE 2-2
Graphic Organizer for
"Matter Particles"

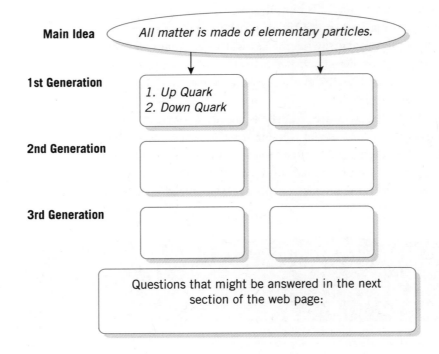

Next, if your purpose is to really understand the information from CERN, you might go back to the web page and reread the material closely. As you read, you might add details to your graphic organizer, such as a vertical line showing how first-generation particles are more stable than second- and third-generation particles. The key here is that the organizer was not the end product; instead, it served as a guide for reading and for close analysis of the text under study. Sometimes students think filling out the organizer is the point of the activity, but most often the organizer is just the visual learning tool that led to learning.

Use Graphic Organizers to Differentiate Instruction

How might that learning be scaffolded using graphic organizers? There are several approaches, but to help you get started thinking, here are some ideas.

1. Provide the organizer in Figure 2-2 to students who have little knowledge of the content and might struggle with the vocabulary or word-level reading tasks.
2. Modify the organizer to include some of the key words and a sample question for students who seem to have some applicable background knowledge of the topic or how it is organized.
3. Challenge students who are close to meeting the content standard to create their own graphic organizer for the passage. This may be more appropriate for older elementary students or for younger students who have used one or two organizers and can make choices about which is most appropriate.

How learning is measured depends on the content and literacy outcomes and standards, a topic to which we return later in this book.

Use Graphic Organizers to Help Students Learn in Each Discipline

Students working with graphic organizers are typically trying to make sense of some content. It could be a science concept (as in our example above), a cause/effect sequence from social studies, a novel with complex characters and plot, and so on. In a sense, the content area doesn't matter: The challenge of understanding something new or at a new level of complexity is the same. For this reason, use any organizer flexibly, as you see fit. That said, occasionally we refer to disciplinary literacy (Moje, 2007; Shanahan & Shanahan, 2008), a way of thinking about literacy tasks that differ from one discipline to another. For example, as teachers we may sometimes show students how to think like a historian or a scientist. The idea is that historians and scientists look at text in their disciplines, whether they are reading or creating it, in different ways. Disciplinary literacies are emphasized more often in the secondary grade levels, but at times it is appropriate for younger students in elementary grades to read like a mathematician or write like a scientist or an author of fiction.

Use Graphic Organizers Digitally or as Hard-Copy Handouts

As you have seen thus far in the book, we like to use both digital graphic organizers and paper organizers that might be hand-drawn or copied for students. Which type you use naturally depends on the grade level you teach (children in K–2 might not yet have sufficient skills to use a computer or tablet) and on your school's access to technology. The following advice, then, is based on the assumption that you have access and, broadly speaking, are working with students in upper elementary grades.

At times it may not matter whether students work on paper or in digital environments (includes tablets, laptops, wearables, desktop computers, and other devices that are often connected to the Internet). At other times, it might be useful to consider the affordances of each. All of the authors of this book are proponents of technology as a means of constructing knowledge, sharing ideas, and making a place in our connected world; however, sometimes we like good, old-fashioned paper, too. What does paper offer?

- **Paper is expandable.** Pieces of paper can be connected together or manipulated. One neat graphic organizer is just 3 × 5 cards laid out on a table in one pattern for a while, then reshuffled and organized a different way. Using large pieces of paper, such as butcher paper, is a good way to track large projects or organize complex ideas with many intricate parts.
- **Paper can be folded** to form an almost infinite variety of organizational patterns. There is something about the kinesthetic task of physically folding paper that appeals to us and to many of the students with whom we have worked over the years.

What are the advantages of digital formats?

- **Digitally created graphic organizers are easily shared.** An organizer created digitally can be shared with other students, parents, or other audiences readily using email, blogs, wikis, and course management systems (e.g., Canvas, eCollege).
- **Digitally created graphic organizers offer creative options** to mash up or include other content via links, embedded media, and the like.
- **A variety of tools are easily adapted for digitally created graphic organizers.** Presentation software, word-processing programs, and drawing programs may all be used to create digital graphic organizers. Of course, many programs are specifically designed for creating graphic organizers as well. The popular Inspiration software is one example.

TIERED ORGANIZERS: SCAFFOLD STUDENT PROGRESS

Throughout the rest of this book, we share organizers we have found useful and encourage you to see how powerful they are as a tool for differentiation (McMackin & Witherell, 2005). This differentiation can be in the form of using them to understand different modes of discourse, for example, the texts students read (Griffin, Malone, & Kameenui, 1995), the texts they compose (e.g., a report), or the "texts" they create through peer and class discussion of challenging ideas and concepts. And as you will see in the Examples of Tiered Graphic Organizers section later in the chapter, tiered graphic organizers can be used to differentiate learners working at different levels of proficiency or command of content. Across the disciplines, they boost knowledge acquisition and independence before, during, and after students encounter challenging texts:

- reading complex texts (DiCecco & Gleason, 2002), including word problems in mathematics (Braselton & Decker, 1994)
- writing from sources (McLaughlin & Overturf, 2013)
- discussing challenging ideas and concepts (Wolsey & Lapp, 2009)

Remember, not every student needs the same graphic organizer at exactly the same time during any instructional sequence. Think about your teaching purposes just as you will later teach them to reflect on students' purposes for using or crafting a graphic. For example, do you want students to make broad-stroke connections? Do you want to help them get an initial overview at the start of a new unit or comprehend an article on new content? Do you want students to use an organizer to make nuanced connections once they have a handle on a topic? Do you want to share an organizer so that students can use it as a precursor to explaining a topic or idea to others? These are the types of questions to consider, and always be mindful of how much students already know, the level of detail they need to know, and how deep a connection you want them to make. All this is background for selecting or using tiered organizers:

- **Advance organizers** (attributed to Ausubel, 1960) are a means of helping students see connections before they engage with a concept or specific material. These organizers are useful when students are engaged with material they are taking in, or receiving. A useful tool, a type of advance organizer, is the structured overview. Suppose that students are entering a class for the first time. The instructor has graphically displayed how the various concepts in the course are related. As a result, students do not see the content as a disconnected set of ideas, but rather as a coherent whole with each idea associated to others. Instead of individual jigsaw pieces, the learners see the whole picture before they begin assembling the puzzle.

- **Partially filled-out organizers** are those in which the teacher has provided a basic structure but also some of the information that helps students see what goes where and why.

- **Blank graphic organizers** provide the bare-bones structure of the ideas, reading material, or other content such that students can see what direction the big picture is taking. However, students must do most of the work of making sense of the material.

- **Student-created or -modified organizers** allow students to make choices, based on their past work with graphic organizers and study guides, about what shape their organizers might take and how they might use them. These are often most useful for students in fifth grade and beyond, who are working on complex composing tasks (e.g., a written product, a multimodal project) or who have a good sense of the general organization of content or reading material.

- **Modified levels of complexity or depth organizers** create a step-wise means of adding depth or complexity to the organizers, which helps students dive more deeply into the content. Later in this chapter, we provide an example of how this modified, or tiered, organizer plan can work.

- **No organizer.** Yes, that's right. Not every student needs to use a graphic organizer just because some or most of their peers may be doing so. In some cases, students have an alternate way of organizing their thinking (and teachers should press students to explain this alternative) or they are familiar enough with the general organization of the content that the organizers become busy work instead of a helpful guide to learning.

Use Graphic Organizers to Promote Independent Thinking and Use

A proficient reader is able to visualize the structure of the text and use this organizational understanding to more deeply comprehend the information the author is sharing. As students become familiar with available graphic organizers, they can immediately make a match between the information shared in a text they are reading and a visual that supports their note-taking as well as later presentations of their related ideas and arguments. Students may need to craft or revise an existing structure to accommodate their intentions.

For example, in a fifth-grade class engaged in closely reading and discussing a text about orbital debris, Emmanuel noted that the author was identifying both a problem and a solution. Isabella chimed in and suggested that they should craft a problem/solution graphic organizer to take their notes while reading and conversing about the text. James added that they would have to add sections to include all of the possible solutions because some had been tested and others were just being hypothesized.

These students were able to engage in this type of thinking and learning independence because they had been introduced to the value of using graphic organizers to support their visualization of information and data. Doing so had become such a natural process for them that intuiting the structure of a text was a significant feature to consider as a part of their text analysis. They were able to move beyond what had been presented to them and create graphics that supported both their learning and presentation of ideas. As this example illustrates, the goal of introducing students to features of various graphic organizers is to support students' independent use and creation of them.

Use Graphic Organizers as Formative Assessment Tools

Graphic organizers provide many assessment opportunities. Dirksen (2011) demonstrates how graphic organizers may be used to provide formative feedback to students as their understanding of academic topics increases. Formative feedback is what the chef does when he tastes the soup (Stake, as quoted by Dirksen, 2011). Once the customer tastes the soup, that's summative assessment. We want our students to have the information about their performance that they need to adjust things as they go instead of waiting until the end to find out how they did. Graphic organizers provide just the venue for students to adjust their own thinking with feedback from the teacher and the organizer itself to know where new learning and ideas can take hold. Because students are novices at the learning—that is why they are students, right?—they need the guidance of experts who know how to question, nudge, prod, or point out what is worthwhile and helpful. We think graphic organizers can help guide students as they construct understandings and make new connections when teachers use them judiciously. We want to help students know when to taste the soup and whom to ask if they are not sure the soup is turning out as expected.

Teachers can best use graphic organizers as formative assessment while the learning is going on, not as a collection of digital or paper organizers turned in after the learning has occurred. What can teachers do?

• First, graphic organizers are often better suited as activities that help students work toward achieving outcomes and standards, and not so much as a gradebook item. They often present a low-risk means of helping students understand without the penalty associated with getting it just the way the teacher wants it.

• Second, graphic organizers are most useful when what students are learning is new, unfamiliar, or in a second language. For that reason, they are guides, not yardsticks.

• Third, in our careers as teachers and professors who work with teachers, we have had the privilege of working with so many fantastic teachers. We have noticed that the most effective teachers are always looking around the classroom, observing, coaching, and nudging. They never "walk and stalk." The moments when their guidance is necessary, planned or unplanned, are where the teaching and learning happens with graphic organizers as one way to make these magic interactions occur.

EXAMPLES OF TIERED GRAPHIC ORGANIZERS

Differentiated instruction meets the needs of all levels of learners in a classroom. Instruction can be modified in content, process, or product (Tomlinson, 1999). The *content* of instruction can be modified to give various levels of learners individualized instruction. The *process* of instruction can be differentiated by grouping students in homogeneous groups so the teacher can instruct the groups based on needed skills. By tiering the *product*, a teacher can plan a lesson and teach it to all students, but modify the way that students show understanding of the content. Teachers cannot feasibly plan small-group or individualized instruction for each lesson; therefore, modifying the product can help meet the needs of individuals if used strategically. Tiered graphic organizers are intended for all types of learners and challenge students' cognitive demand in any subject area.

Example: Science

One adaptation of tiered graphic organizers is giving students a choice of how to represent information they've learned. Students choose a concept map to represent the information collected. In 1972, Novak "developed" concept maps while he was researching ways to help students understand science (Novak & Musonda 1991).

Students create or can be given content vocabulary cards, which they then organize on a table. Then, students draw this representation on paper (see Figure 2-3). The teacher can assess students' analytical and synthesizing skills. For instance, the teacher can assess students' conceptual understanding of whether the water cycle is linear or cyclical. Another option would be to give students a choice of graphic organizers by previously modeling each organizer's use and providing copies of various organizers during or after a lesson.

Example: Social Studies

A more structured way to use tiered organizers, instead of giving students free choice, is to group students into homogeneous groups. Each group receives a graphic organizer that is tiered to the group's overall ability. In social studies, for example, students may collect facts about the Roman Empire. One group might be responsible for completing a circle map

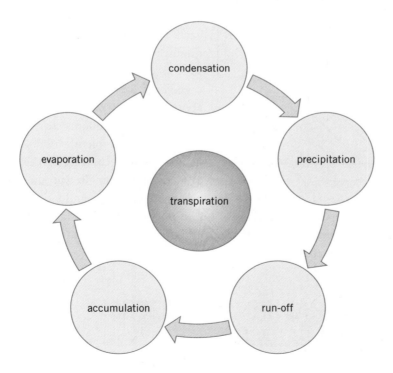

FIGURE 2-3
The Water Cycle

**FIGURE 2-3
(Continued)**

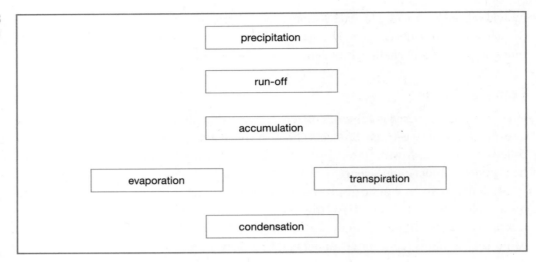

**FIGURE 2-4
Circle Map**

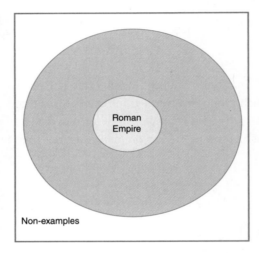

**FIGURE 2-5
Partial Herringbone
Timeline**

of the culture (Figure 2-4). An intermediate group might complete a timeline. A high-achieving group might complete a herringbone organizer, showing the main characteristics, as well as details for each (Figure 2-5).

To extend this activity, students from two groups could compare graphic organizers to discuss the benefits and downfalls of using each type. This will help students begin to choose appropriate situations in which to use each type of organizer. Another extension might be to teach about another culture, such as Greek culture, and have students use tiered organizers that illustrate understanding about new and previously learned cultures. For example, students in the circle map group could complete a double bubble map, comparing and contrasting the two cultures. Students in the timeline group could complete a double timeline. And students in the herringbone group could complete a double herringbone to compare and contrast. This could then extend into a discussion about the common characteristics of the cultures, their similar strengths and weaknesses, and situations contributing to each (Clarke, 1994).

ADAPTING GRAPHIC ORGANIZERS FOR TIERED LEARNING

- Choose a skill, strategy, or concept you plan to teach.
- Determine the desired outcome for all students after receiving instruction.

- Consider students' level. Instruction should not be too easy or at a level that will cause frustration.
- Starting with your advanced students, design a graphic organizer that will help them think more complexly about the strategy.
- Using the same desired outcome, create two less cognitively challenging graphic organizers.
- Using previously collected data, group your students into achievement groups closely related to the skill you are teaching. Consider using a pretest or a formative assessment to help create the groups.
- Give each group the appropriate graphic organizer.
- Assess students' work and encourage them to advance to a more complex organizer when they are ready.
- Encourage students to add dimensions that support any ideas they may have that extend beyond the features of the existing graphic organizer.

A SAMPLE TIERED LESSON

Interactive Picture Book Read Aloud

CCSS.ELA-Literacy.RL.4.1.
Refer to details and examples in a text when explaining what the text says explicitly and when drawing inferences from the text.

CCSS.ELA-Literacy.RL.4.2.
Determine a theme of a story, drama, or poem from details in the text; summarize the text.

CCSS.ELA-Literacy.RL.4.3.
Describe in depth a character, setting, or event in a story or drama, drawing on specific details in the text (e.g., a character's thoughts, words, or actions).

THIS SAMPLE LESSON ADDRESSES THESE STANDARDS

Interactive read-alouds are a way to model your thinking to students and motivate readers to try new texts. Choose a picture book or novel you are reading together in class. You can use think-alouds to scaffold instruction in such a way that students will be able to "copy" the way you think through a text. You can also use tiered questions in your instruction to scaffold for students as they prepare to complete the tiered graphic organizer at the end of the lesson. Graphic organizers can help make an abstract idea like inferring more concrete and, therefore, easier for all students to understand (McMackin & Witherell, 2005).

The Stranger by Chris Van Allsburg (1986) is a picture book in which the reader must infer to figure out who the mysterious character is. As you read this text to your students, think aloud to model your inferring. For example:

As I was reading, I noticed the author gives many clues to help us figure out who the stranger is. He says, 'The man on the sofa was dressed in odd, rough leather clothing.' He describes how he tries to run off, loses his balance, and falls. Van Allsburg also gives us clues about how he 'seemed confused about buttonholes and buttons' and that 'the steam that rose from the hot food fascinated him.' Good readers put clues together to make inferences about a character. As you read, you should look for clues and think about what you've figured out. As I read the rest of the book, write down clues that you think are important in your graphic organizer.

Students' graphic organizers can be tiered by asking the students who are higher achieving with this content and text type to make more inferences and cite more text evidence to support the inferences. Struggling students have fewer requirements for making inferences and citing textual evidence. Notice how the organizers in Figures 2-6, 2-7, and 2-8 differ in structure.

At this point, the teacher can collect the graphic organizers and assess each student. Alternatively, inferences and textual evidence can be shared on a class graphic organizer and students can add spaces to their graphic organizers. Be sure to encourage students to support their inferences from the text. Making text-to-graphic connections promotes students' independence as they begin to visualize how their ideas can best be represented and displayed.

FIGURE 2-6
Introductory-Level Graphic Organizer for Making Inferences

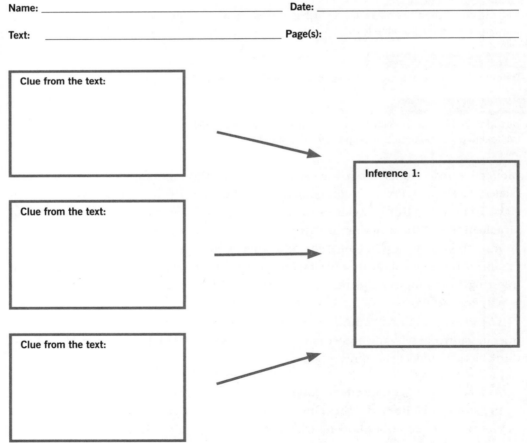

Name: _____ Date: _____

Text: _____ Page(s): _____

FIGURE 2-7
Intermediate-Level
Graphic Organizer for
Making Inferences

Clue from the text:	Clue from the text:	Clue from the text:

Inference 1:

Clue from the text:	Clue from the text:	Clue from the text:

Inference 2:

FIGURE 2-8
Advanced-Level
Graphic Organizer for
Making Inferences

Name: _____ Date: _____

Text: _____ Page(s): _____

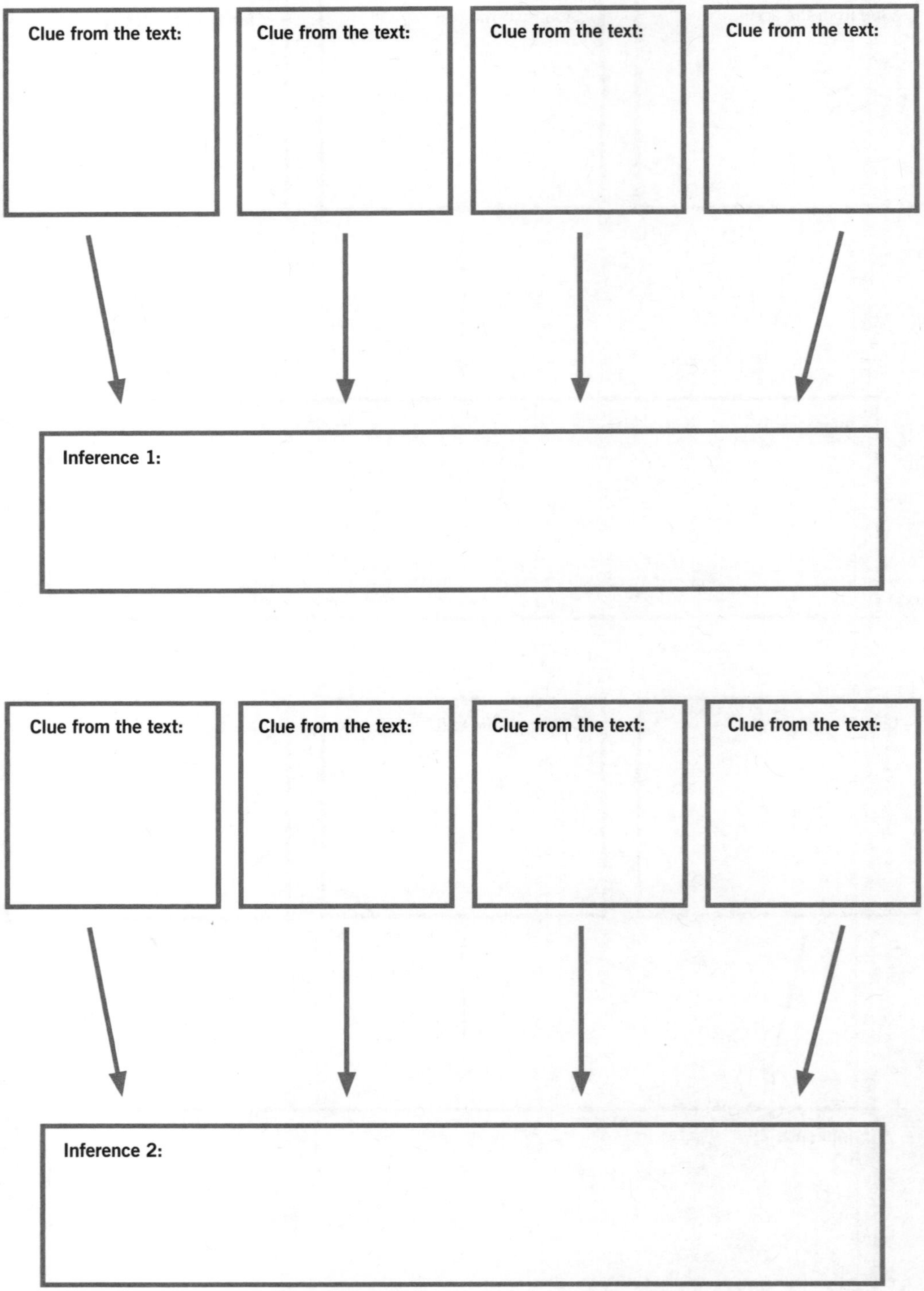

| Clue from the text: | Clue from the text: | Clue from the text: | Clue from the text: |

Inference 1:

| Clue from the text: | Clue from the text: | Clue from the text: | Clue from the text: |

Inference 2:

AT-A-GLANCE CHART OF GRAPHIC ORGANIZERS MATCHED TO ACADEMIC GOALS

We close this chapter with a recap. Research from education and neuroscience has shown why graphic organizers are so "brain-friendly" to young learners (or any learners). There are a handful of general tips for selecting and developing graphic organizers in the most effective ways. These tips seem to distill into a simple truth: To use them well, know your students and your teaching purposes.

Now, before you turn to the "how to" chapters, we share a matrix so you have a big-picture view of what lies ahead. In the following chapters, you will find many examples of graphic organizers we have used along with sample lessons or examples, each linked to Common Core State Standards. This matrix shows the graphic organizers by chapter (also see the Appendix for a matrix showing the organizers aligned with eight academic skills).

Chapter 3: Using Graphic Organizers to Acquire Academic Vocabulary	Frayer Organzer Concept/Definition Map Word Map
Chapter 4: Graphic Organizers Support Literary Text Reading and Writing Tasks	Character Graphic Freytag's Pyramid
Chapter 5: Graphic Organizers Support Informational Text Reading and Writing Tasks	Text Search and Find Board 4-Square With a Diamond Modified KWL Tabbed Book Manipulative
Chapter 6: Graphic Organizers Support Students' Reading Proficiencies	Somebody-Wanted-But-So Understanding Text Structures (sequential, descriptive, cause/effect, compare and contrast, problem/solution)
Chapter 7: Graphic Organizers Boost Questioning and Responding	I-Chart and I-Guide Flip Chart Manipulative Text-Dependent Question/Response Organizer
Chapter 8: Graphic Organizers Foster Reading, Forming, and Writing Opinions	Six-Part Opinion Chart Thinking Map
Chapter 9: Graphic Organizers Support Collaboration	Project Management Organizer

USING GRAPHIC ORGANIZERS TO ACQUIRE ACADEMIC VOCABULARY

Teaching students to comprehend and use the language of school and the various disciplines is certainly a Common Core State Standard (CCSS) shift that is also a goal of every teacher. Graphic organizers offer major support in this knowledge and language acquisition by providing an organizing visual that helps to illustrate academic terminology within a viewed context that supports developing a deep understanding of the term, its meaning, and its contextual family. Let's consider how the following organizers support a deepened understanding and use of academic language.

FRAYER ORGANIZER

CCSS.ELA-Literacy.CCRA.L.4.

Determine or clarify the meaning of unknown and multiple-meaning words and phrases by using context clues, analyzing meaningful word parts, and consulting general and specialized reference materials, as appropriate.

CCSS.ELA-Literacy.CCRA.L.5.

Demonstrate understanding of figurative language, word relationships, and nuances in word meanings.

CCSS.ELA-Literacy.CCRA.L.6.

Acquire and use accurately a range of general academic and domain-specific words and phrases sufficient for reading, writing, speaking, and listening at the college and career readiness level; demonstrate independence in gathering vocabulary knowledge when encountering an unknown term important to comprehension or expression.

THIS ORGANIZER ADDRESSES THESE STANDARDS

What Is the Frayer Organizer?

The Frayer organizer (Figure 3-1) is intended to be used as an in-class activity that capitalizes on the interactions students have with sources and with each other as they learn concepts, usually represented as a vocabulary term. If the Frayer is simply given to students as homework (IRIS Center, n.d.), the value of the discussion is lost. The Frayer organizer helps students go beyond definitions and look at the attributes of a given concept.

FIGURE 3-1
Frayer Organizer

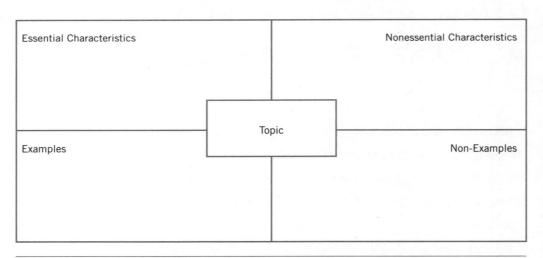

Essential Characteristics	Nonessential Characteristics
Examples	**Topic**	Non-Examples

Source: Adapted from the original Frayer Model, created by Dorothy Frayer, University of Wisconsin.

How Do I Use a Frayer Organizer?

• You, the teacher, determine which terms you want your students to explore. The terms should be critical to understanding the reading students will do, the videos they may see, and the writing they will do.

- Next, provide students with accessible definitions of the terms, or students may consult student-friendly resources to find their own appropriate definitions. (Alternatively, you can provide just enough context to help students find a reasonable definition on their own.)

- Students work in pairs or small groups to complete the remainder of the organizer, adding examples, characteristics, and non-examples.

- Circulate as students work, providing support where needed. Sometimes coming up with non-examples can be difficult for students, so be prepared to offer a model of how to do it. Tip off students that useful non-examples often share attributes with examples. For example, a peach and a plum share attributes, yet a peach is a non-example of a plum. By contrast, saying that a rock is a non-example of a plum doesn't contribute useful information. So guide students to learn to identify the *relevant* attributes of the examples and non-examples, then indicate why the non-examples are helpful.

- Let students know when it is okay to adapt information. For example, instead of naming characteristics, students might illustrate the concept or term or find an image of it online. If they can't find a representation, invite them to create one. This promotes their independent use of the graphic.

- Consider digital tools as a means for students to share work with parents, other students, and you. Students can refer to each other's digital Frayer organizers to reinforce or adjust their learning if they are shared on a class web page or blog.

INTO THE CLASSROOM

Fifth Grade—U.S. Government

CCSS.ELA-LITERACY.RI.5.1.
Quote accurately from a text when explaining what the text says explicitly and when drawing inferences from the text.

CCSS.ELA-LITERACY.RI.5.4.
Determine the meaning of general academic and domain-specific words and phrases in a text relevant to a grade 5 topic or subject area.

CCSS.ELA-LITERACY.RI.5.7.
Draw on information from multiple print or digital sources, demonstrating the ability to locate an answer to a question quickly or to solve a problem efficiently.

CCSS.ELA-LITERACY.RI.5.9.
Integrate information from several texts on the same topic in order to write or speak about the subject knowledgeably.

THIS CLASSROOM EXAMPLE ADDRESSES THESE STANDARDS

Determining the Need[1]

Mrs. Carter introduced her fifth-grade students to the foundation of the U.S. government and the important documents that helped define our democracy. Later, they would read materials that include the words they explored through the Frayer model. She made a list of seven key vocabulary words she expected students to know in order for them to grasp the concepts presented in the unit. Students may have had previous knowledge of some of the words, but through an anticipation guide Mrs. Carter realized students did not have a deep understanding of the words.

Introducing It

Mrs. Carter introduced the new vocabulary on a whiteboard, making sure to pronounce each of the words for students before they begin. The vocabulary words she used were *republic, ratify, compromise, amendment, citizens, commerce,* and *government.* She let students know the importance of each of the vocabulary words in order to understand the upcoming unit. Next, Mrs. Carter showed the class the digital Frayer organizer, explaining each of its parts. Using a template created through the software Prezi, Mrs. Carter used the word *executive* to think aloud the process of filling out the digital Frayer. Since Prezi allows users to upload cited photos through Google, Mrs. Carter showed the simplicity of the program to students.

FIGURE 3-2
Digital Frayer *Republic* Example Using Prezi

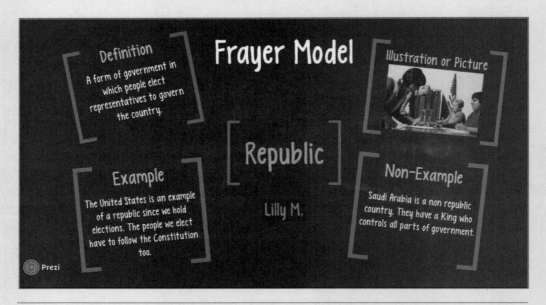

Source: Contributed by Lindsay Merritt. Photo used with permission of Thinkstock/Digital Vision.

Guided and Independent Practice

Following the example, Mrs. Carter gave students one of the seven vocabulary words to look up, and they began their research. Students were asked to complete a digital Frayer using the template provided on Prezi. Students were able to use the textbook as well as online resources such as glossaries, webquests, and encyclopedias to find their vocabulary

---

1. The lesson model used in this book is based on the work of Madeline Hunter (1982) and adjusted for our purposes.

word. After completing the digital Frayer independently, Mrs. Carter asked students to meet with the other students who had their same word. She asked these small groups to read the textbook section in which the word appears and explain how their definition compared with the usage of the word in the text.

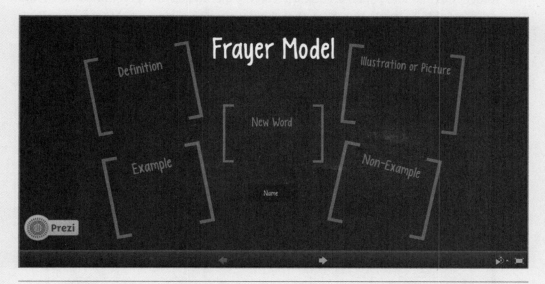

FIGURE 3-3
Digital Frayer Template
Using Prezi

Source: Contributed by Lindsay Merritt.

Closure

Students came together as a class. Mrs. Carter allowed them to come to the whiteboard and share individual digital Frayer organizers. Since some of the students had the same word, Mrs. Carter asked the class to look at the charts and compare where each student's ideas were the same or different. After an open discussion of the new vocabulary, Mrs. Carter asked students to think about how the words connected to the reading they had completed earlier or how they might relate to the unit they were studying.

Reading, Writing, and Discussion Extensions

One of the benefits of the Frayer organizer is that it allows teachers to intervene when they intuit that, despite reading and discussion, students have a shaky grasp of important terms. The organizer gives students the time to "steep" themselves in a term they've already come up against, apply their findings to authentic text, and then refine and share new knowledge with peers. And as we have seen, the organizer gives students a running start on comprehension of texts they are about to read. We also really like the built-in collaborative piece, which is a great match-up to the kind of collaborative work recommended by the Common Core. When students are given the chance to practice newly acquired vocabulary in conversation, it boosts their academic speech and nourishes their academic writing skills. It also provides them with opportunities to add new dimensions to any organizer they are using or are planning to create.

Students Create Their Own

The Frayer graphic also works well as a handwritten tool. Figure 3-4 shows Eli's Frayer creation for the term *accelerate* from his science reading. Because the Frayer has four quadrants, with a circle or square in the middle where students write the terms they are to learn, it is easy to recreate on blank paper as a manipulative organizer, too. Just fold the paper into fourths and write the word in the middle to avoid the copy machine. We find that students like to fold paper, and light-colored paper makes the assignment more fun. Using this graphic helps them realize that they can manipulate or create a new graphic that shows the intent of their learning or message.

FIGURE 3-4
Handwritten Frayer for
Accelerate

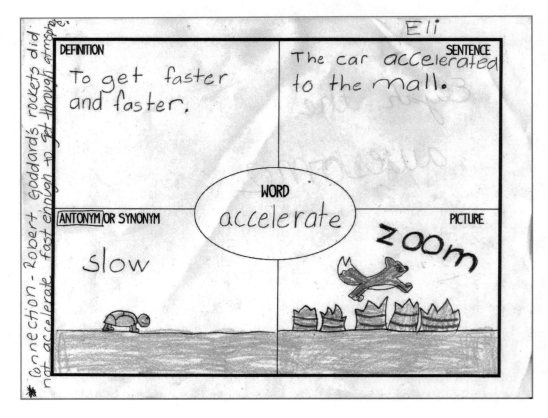

CONCEPT/DEFINITION MAP

Determine or clarify the meaning of unknown and multiple-meaning words and phrases by using context clues, analyzing meaningful word parts, and consulting general and specialized reference materials, as appropriate.

Demonstrate understanding of figurative language, word relationships, and nuances in word meanings.

THIS ORGANIZER ADDRESSES THESE STANDARDS

What Is a Concept/Definition Map?

A concept/definition map (Figure 3-5) (first conceived of by Schwartz and Raphael in 1985 as a Concept of Definition Map) is typically a bubble-type format. At the center is the central concept or term, surrounded by three bubbles containing key questions provided by the teacher: *What is it? What is it like? What are some examples?* These questions jump-start students to activate what they know about the term and to look for relevant details and answers. A final section of the graphic helps students synthesize the information and then rephrase it into their own written definitions.

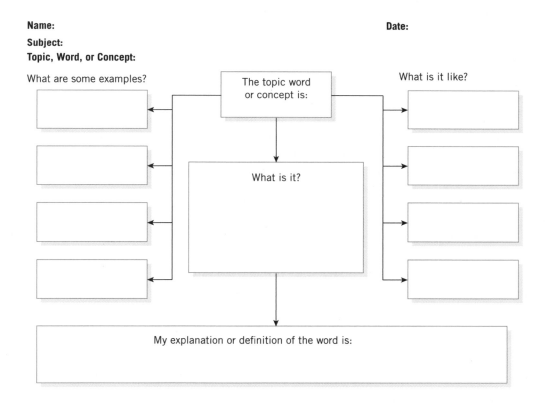

FIGURE 3-5
Concept/Definition Map

The overarching goal is for students to know to make richer connections to any term or concept (really, terms often either describe or relate to concepts) and, by doing so, to deepen their understanding. Schwartz and Raphael (1985) developed the method because they saw that when students encountered a new term, they needed a way to explore and organize their current knowledge in order to then better determine what additional information they needed to expand their understanding of the meaning(s). These two educators had observed that the traditional look-it-up-in-the-dictionary approach did little to deepen students' word and concept knowledge.

How Do I Use a Concept/Definition Map?

- You will need chart paper, a software program, and a way to display the map; perhaps with a document camera on a whiteboard. Each student will need a copy of the reproducible or a blank piece of copy paper.
- Choose the topic, concept, or vocabulary term that might be confusing to your students or one they may need to more deeply understand.
- Display your version of the chart with the topic in the center surrounded by the three key questions:
  - What is it?
  - What is it like?
  - What are some examples?
- The ensuing discussion can be conducted with the entire class, in small groups, or even individually. Students should draw on their own background knowledge about the topic, but then expand their search by investigating assigned texts and other online sources that support their responding to the key questions.
- Students then complete the fourth area of the organizer by writing their own definition or explanation of the topic, word, or concept. ("Concept/Definition Maps to Comprehend Curriculum Content," 2011).
- *Variations*: A variation on this idea from Gill (2007) suggests using this bubble-type organizer to place a term in the center and then use the surrounding bubbles to break down the word itself into parts. For example, students might be asked to break the word into syllables or list in the surrounding bubbles words that have the same root or affix. In Gill's organizer, students use Kidspiration to include both text and images as they explore vocabulary.

Websites That Provide an Outlet for Concept/Definition Maps

- www.prezi.com: This program allows users to create a graphic organizer using bubbles, shapes, and text, and to navigate through it easily. Pictures, music, and graphics can be added to enhance the organizer.

- www.padlet.com: With this program a teacher or student can post a main idea (vocabulary word) and other students can attach "sticky note" type boxes around the word. This is a great way to collaborate.

CCSS.ELA-Literacy.RI.4.1.

Refer to details and examples in a text when explaining what the text says explicitly and when drawing inferences from the text.

CCSS.ELA-Literacy.RI.4.4.

Determine the meaning of general academic and domain-specific words or phrases in a text relevant to a grade 4 topic or subject area.

CCSS.ELA-Literacy.SL.4.1.

Engage effectively in a range of collaborative discussions (one-on-one, in groups, and teacher-led) with diverse partners on grade 4 topics and texts, building on others' ideas and expressing their own clearly.

THIS CLASSROOM EXAMPLE ADDRESSES THESE STANDARDS

Determining the Need

Fourth graders in Ms. Walker's class were classifying and studying various types of rocks. Through a brief class discussion, Mrs. Walker determined that students had a contextual knowledge of the word *composition*, but that was it. She knew that if they didn't fully understand the term, it would make it tougher to grasp related concepts. Ms. Walker selected a concept/definition map, knowing that it would deepen students' understanding of the term and be a boon to their comprehension of the readings throughout the unit. Her goal was to have them understand the term well enough to use it in their academic discussions and in their written work, and be able to understand its nuances in different text contexts.

Introducing It

Ms. Walker introduced the concept/definition map during a whole-class discussion of rocks, using a whiteboard and a handout of the concept/definition map on the word *composition*. She began by asking students to record the word on their map as she wrote it on the whiteboard. Students then followed along with Ms. Walker as she gave an example of an informational text that contained *composition* in relation to rock formation. As she read aloud, students filled in the first boxes on each side of the organizer. Once Ms. Walker completed the reading, students did a "turn and talk" with a classmate to share the information they had gained about *composition* from the reading.

Guided and Independent Practice

Ms. Walker checked for understanding as students worked, gauging not only their knowledge of the term, but also how well they were handling the concept/definition map. Most students seemed to be using the information from the text she'd read aloud to articulate additional concepts related to composition, so she invited the class to read their current leveled reader, also on rock formation, and add to their map any new information they came across. Ms. Walker used this time to pull together a small group of students who needed extra support, and together they worked on the concept/ definition map so she could reinforce procedures and help them build confidence with the word learning task.

FIGURE 3-6
Students' Concept/
Definition Map

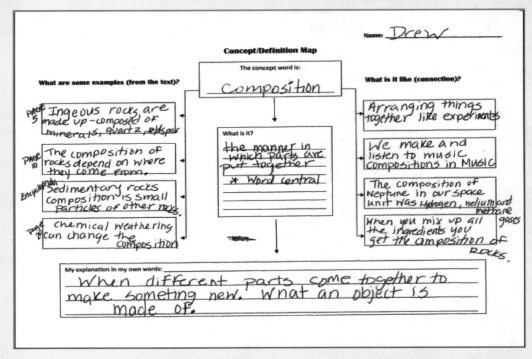

Closure

Once the pages are assembled, the book can be put into the classroom library for continuous reading throughout the year. The students and teacher can look back to make connections to future units or reference when learning comparable vocabulary.

Reading, Writing, and Discussion Extensions

Once students have developed a reasonable concept of definition for a given word, they can be expected to use these terms in their written work and in discussion. Their usage may still be somewhat unsophisticated, but that is okay. The more students use terms representing difficult or challenging concepts, the more likely they will be to become proficient and conversant with the term. When students use concept/definition maps to increase their knowledge of a word or concept, they are initially drawing on their own experiences, but this is where the learning begins, not ends. As they explore additional sources they experience new ways of using the term, which promotes an expanded conceptualization of its meaning. You might adjust this chart so that students can indicate the source(s) of the information they consulted with and an explanation sharing how the source(s) expanded owning the word.

A useful way for students to demonstrate this new vocabulary knowledge is to have them create a Class Informational Guide using the vocabulary they have learned throughout the unit of study. Students can work in pairs or individually to create a page that will be entered into the classroom book. Each student is considered an "expert" in her or his field and uses the newly obtained vocabulary. Students include a paragraph or page (whichever is grade-level-appropriate) demonstrating their understanding of the word according to the information they gained using the concept/definition map. Students can include a picture or diagram to show understanding and any other information that relates to the newly learned vocabulary.

WORD MAP

Contributed by Lindsay Merritt

CCSS.ELA-Literacy.CCRA.L.4.

Determine or clarify the meaning of unknown and multiple-meaning words and phrases by using context clues, analyzing meaningful word parts, and consulting general and specialized reference materials, as appropriate.

CCSS.ELA-Literacy.CCRA.L.5.

Demonstrate understanding of figurative language, word relationships, and nuances in word meanings.

CCSS.ELA-Literacy.CCRA.L.6.

Acquire and use accurately a range of general academic and domain-specific words and phrases sufficient for reading, writing, speaking, and listening at the college and career readiness level; demonstrate independence in gathering vocabulary knowledge when encountering an unknown term important to comprehension or expression.

THIS ORGANIZER ADDRESSES THESE STANDARDS

What Is a Word Map?

A word map (Figure 3-7) is a graphic organizer with space for definitions, synonyms, words and sentences in context, and pictures or symbols, somewhat similar to a Frayer organizer and a concept/definition map. Students can complete these for vocabulary terms that are important in a given lesson individually or as groups. The word map format allows

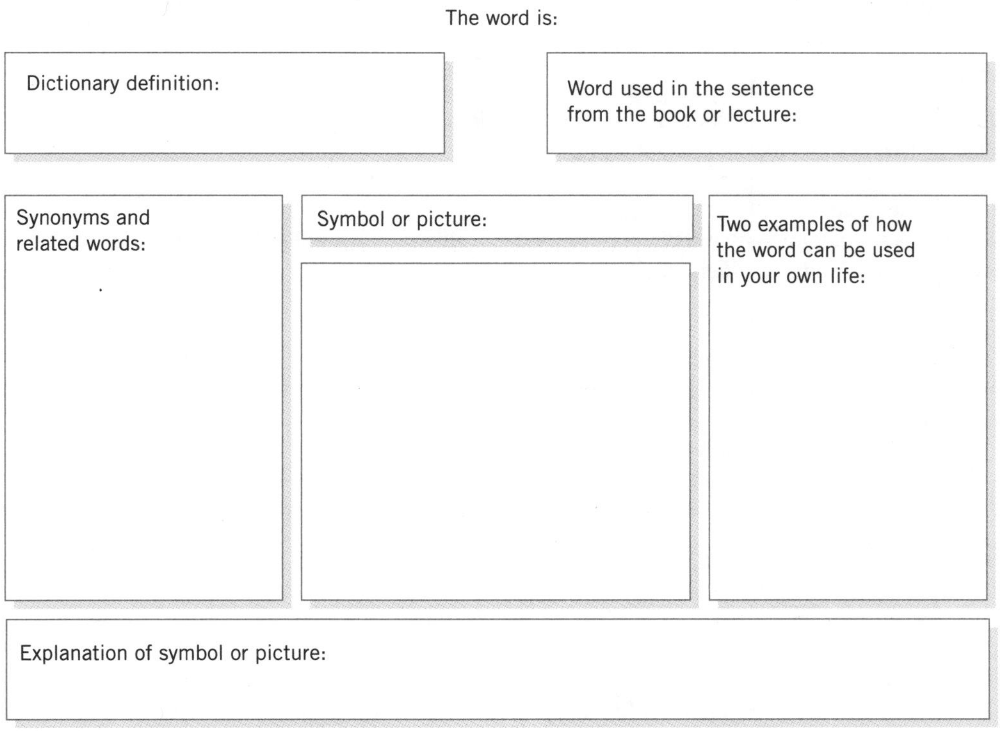

FIGURE 3-7
Word Map

The word is:

| Dictionary definition: | Word used in the sentence from the book or lecture: |

| Synonyms and related words: | Symbol or picture: | Two examples of how the word can be used in your own life: |

Explanation of symbol or picture:

students to reinforce their understanding of the concept represented by the vocabulary by looking at it in a number of different ways. Students' background knowledge is enhanced because they are encouraged to make connections to prior knowledge and experience.

How Do I Use a Word Map ?

• Choose target terms students should learn. These should be tier two words (Beck, McKeown, & Kucan, 2002) that are academic in nature but cut across content areas or tier three words that are specific to a given content area or discipline.

• If a single term is the target, students might work independently. If there are several terms, students may work in groups focused on one of the words, or they may each take ownership of one of the words.

• After students have completed the map, have them share their understanding and examples with other members of the group or with the class. Through discussion and group presentation, they build on the knowledge gained from completing the graphic organizer.

Word maps can easily be adapted for use with digital resources such as Google Drive, PowerPoint, or Prezi, or they can be used traditionally with a whiteboard or chart paper.

INTO THE CLASSROOM

Third Grade—Space

THIS CLASSROOM EXAMPLE ADDRESSES THESE STANDARDS

CCSS.ELA-Literacy.RI.3.4.

Determine the meaning of general academic and domain-specific words and phrases in a text relevant to a grade 3 topic or subject area.

CCSS.ELA-Literacy.RI.3.5.

Use text features and search tools (e.g., key words, sidebars, hyperlinks) to locate information relevant to a given topic efficiently.

CCSS.ELA-Literacy.SL.3.1.

Engage effectively in a range of collaborative discussions (one-on-one, in groups, and teacher-led) with diverse partners on grade 3 topics and texts, building on others' ideas and expressing their own clearly.

CCSS.ELA-Literacy.L.3.4d.

Use glossaries or beginning dictionaries, both print and digital, to determine or clarify the precise meaning of key words and phrases.

Determining the Need

Third-grade teacher Mr. Martinez was launching a study on the solar system and the space race to the moon. In the first week he and students read a few chapters of the biography *Rocket Man* about Robert Goddard. He decided to introduce the word map organizer as a way to give his students a firm grasp of terms he knew would cause difficulty for them.

Introducing It

Mr. Martinez reviewed the main ideas and important details of the reading they had been doing over the past week. He introduced the new vocabulary on a pocket chart in the classroom. Mr. Martinez chose six key vocabulary words that students would encounter in the next chapter of *Rocket Man*.

Guided and Independent Practice

Mr. Martinez displayed the word map on the whiteboard, using a template created with Prezi. He explained each part of the map using an example from the text. Students were asked to follow along with Mr. Martinez's word map and ask any questions as they went through.

Following the example, Mr. Martinez released the class to their reading rotation stations that featured different literacy learning tasks. During the vocabulary rotation, students were asked to complete a word map on one of the vocabulary words in the pocket chart. Students were allowed to use features of the text such as the glossary and index to find words and look at the context of the words. Some students chose to use a student dictionary to look up the word and then write in their own words. After completing the word map independently, using the one vocabulary word, students in each reading group (four students per station) discussed the meaning of their word and displayed their word map. Students used this time to compare charts and think through any connections they may have noticed between the vocabulary.

Closure

Students came together as a class after each group had been through the reading rotation. Mr. Martinez encouraged students to share their vocabulary words by showing their word map to the class. Several of the students had the same word, so Mr. Martinez asked the class to look at the charts and compare where each student's ideas were the same or different. After an open discussion of the new vocabulary, Mr. Martinez asked students to think about the connection these words might have to the next chapter in the text. On the back of their maps, students wrote a one sentence prediction on what they felt the chapter would discuss.

Reading, Writing, and Discussion Extensions

Word maps give students the opportunity to explore important terms before or after reading to deepen their knowledge of the word. Through the written aspects of the word map, students further work with the term, then illustrate it. Finally, their written and illustrated work becomes the foundation for discussion during which they use the term in context. As a result, students become more conversant with the term and may employ it more fluently as they understand the concept underlying the word. Students can use a combination of vocabulary words to create sentences, paragraphs, or even stories focused on the vocabulary words. Classroom dictionaries can be created using each of the word maps to reference terms during the unit of study. These extensions illustrate how students go beyond the initial graphic with expansions that illustrate their growing independence as language learners. New vocabulary words can be added, and dictionaries can be referenced throughout the year.

Photo by Thinkstock

GRAPHIC ORGANIZERS SUPPORT LITERARY TEXT READING AND WRITING TASKS

Literary texts differ in several ways from informational texts. In addition to being fictional works, they follow a narrative structure that informational texts may not. Characters and plot development lead to an understanding of the overall theme of the work as well. The following organizers are especially well suited to scaffolding student understanding of literary text.

CHARACTER GRAPHIC

Contributed by Joyce Farrow

THIS ORGANIZER ADDRESSES THESE STANDARDS

CCSS.ELA-Literacy.CCRA.R.2.

Determine central ideas or themes of a text and analyze their development; summarize the key supporting details and ideas.

CCSS.ELA-Literacy.CCRA.R.3.

Analyze how and why individuals, events, or ideas develop and interact over the course of a text.

What Is a Character Graphic?

FIGURE 4-1
Character Graphic

Name: _____

Title: _____ **Author:** _____

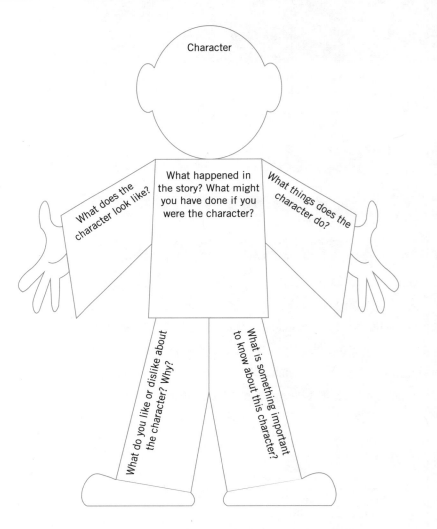

Source: Adapted from *Character Connections,* Florida Center for Reading Research, 2007.

Identifying with characters leads to deeper understanding of story (Bluestein, 2013) and also oneself. Whether evaluating a character's personality or analyzing a character's life, problems, situations, feelings, or actions, the use of characterization encourages students to interact with text, which furthers their comprehension of the story. Incorporating a graphic organizer (such as the one in Figure 4-1) helps "students not only to 'read' and comprehend more easily complex information and relationships but also to generate ideas, structure their thoughts, and learn how to make visible, in an easy-to-read way, what they know" (Birbili, 2006, p. 2). The characterization strategy and use of a graphic organizer lends itself to cross-curricular use especially when connecting subjects such as English language arts and social studies.

Examples of graphic organizers that may be used for characterization where two characters or topics are presented for study are pictured below. Figure 4-2 is more suited to younger students. Figure 4-3 would be more appropriate for older students (Florida Center for Reading Research, n.d.); they are adapted to include additional characters or topics for comparison as well.

How Do I Use a Character Graphic?

• Choose a narrative text (or an informational text with a narrative structure, such as a biography, or a focused text on a concept such as caste systems) that challenges student readers.

Name: _____

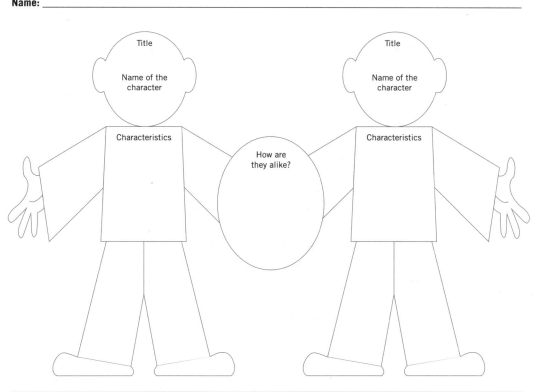

FIGURE 4-2
Character Graphic for Younger Students

Source: Adapted from *Character Connections*, Florida Center for Reading Research, 2007.

FIGURE 4-3
Character Graphic for
Upper Elementary
Students

Name: _____

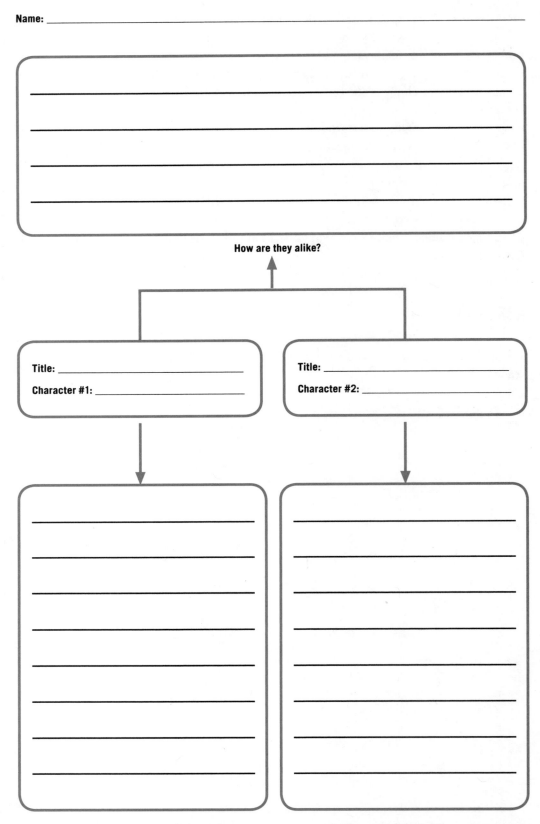

How are they alike?

Title: _____

Character #1: _____

Title: _____

Character #2: _____

Source: Adapted from *Character Connections*, Florida Center for Reading Research, 2007.

- Model how to complete the graphic organizer both during and after reading. With younger students, this may be done several times, scaffolding the process with a gradual release of responsibility before having students use the strategy independently. Older students will also need initial modeling, but they may need fewer teacher-led examples before moving to independent use of the strategy.

- When graduating to making a comparison of characters or topics, provide a few texts on the same topic (a biography and a historical fiction text on a person or a few texts on religious conflicts). Encourage students to visualize their own representations as a way to move them toward more independent thinking and creation.

- Model how to complete the graphic organizer during and after reading, and emphasize noting similarities and/or differences between characters. With upper elementary students, use the organizer to scaffold discussion of character complexity, contradictory traits, and character change. Encourage them to add components to the graphic as needed to show their interpretation or to craft an alternate visual that they feel might better capture the complexity of the character(s).

- Take the strategy a step further by demonstrating to students how to use the information on the organizer to develop a written response. Students can use the information to write a description of a character, to compare two or more characters, or to synthesize several texts on the same topic.

INTO THE CLASSROOM

Second Grade—Historical Figures

CCSS.ELA-Literacy.W.2.2.

Write informative/explanatory texts in which they introduce a topic, use facts and definitions to develop points, and provide a concluding statement or section.

CCSS.ELA-Literacy.W.2.8.

Recall information from experiences or gather information from provided sources to answer a question.

THIS CLASSROOM EXAMPLE ADDRESSES THESE STANDARDS

Determining the Need

Mrs. Farrow's third graders were reading informational texts to gather information about a historical figure they'd each selected. The reading would lead to their writing a report that conveyed key details. Mrs. Farrow set aside several days for reading, completing the organizers, writing a first draft, and completing the writing process. She and her students had framed a question that guided their reading and research: How does a famous person in history shape how we live today? She knew that her students would get overwhelmed by the sheer amount of information in their reading and that if they could lean on the structure of an organizer it would help a lot. Her students were familiar with the graphic organizer; they'd used it while reading and discussing fiction. She recognized, however, that they wouldn't be able to transfer that knowledge to using it with nonfiction and biographies, so she devoted 15 minutes to model how she used one.

Introducing It

Mrs. Farrow conducted a think-aloud and invited students' questions as she used the character graphic during reading. She then modeled how to go back to the graphic after reading to add key details. When she saw that students seemed to have the hang of how it works, she instructed them to work in groups or to read their books and complete their graphic organizers.

Guided and Independent Practice

Mrs. Farrow circulated among the groups, providing support. The next day, she modeled for students how to take the information from the completed graphic organizer and use it to write a draft of their essay. She pointed out that the written text should introduce the person, use facts to develop key points, and provide a concluding statement.

Students again worked in groups (or pairs) to write their essays. She had them share their essays with the class, and then they published them in a class anthology.

Closure

To wrap up, Mrs. Farrow had each student discuss with a partner or in groups one fact he or she learned about a historical figure.

Reading, Writing, and Discussion Extensions

Throughout the Character Graphics sample lesson, students use the fiction or narrative nonfiction they read to more closely scrutinize the texts they encounter. They work in groups to share what they have learned and then use the information to write an introduction about the character. Facts are the foundation of research and inquiry stances. A possible connection of the character graphic is Freytag's pyramid, which links plot structures and characterization (see the next section).

FREYTAG'S PYRAMID

THIS ORGANIZER EXAMPLE ADDRESSES THESE STANDARDS

What Is a Freytag's Pyramid?

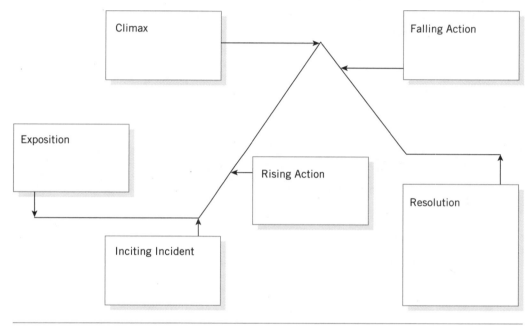

FIGURE 4-4
Freytag's Pyramid

Source: Adapted from Holman and Harmon, 1992.

Freytag's pyramid (Figure 4-4) is a diagram first published in 1863 that is intended to explain a five-act tragedy, and it is named after Gustav Freytag (Holman & Harmon, 1992). Since that time, the diagram has been applied to many different types of fiction. We have found it makes the task of summarizing short stories and novels a little easier for students. The text of it is easily adapted for younger students.

How Do I Use a Freytag's Pyramid?

• Make sure students know the elements of literature required to complete the Freytag's pyramid graphic organizer. For primary-age students, it could be as simple as beginning, middle, and ending; character; and problem/challenge. For students in fifth grade, the elements might include terms such as *plot, rising action,* and *dénouement.*

- Spend 10–15 minutes modeling how you complete the pyramid, or fill one out with students.

- Then have students fill in the pyramid while they read a short story or novel. This scaffolds their understanding of the structure of the story, and the notes they jot down will help them recall and summarize later.

- You might also ask students to complete the pyramid after reading a story or novel as a way of assessing their understanding.

- We have found that an effective practice is to have students complete a rough draft of the pyramid on their own, then work on chart paper or an interactive website. An online version can be found if you navigate to www.readwritethink.org/resources/resource-print.html?id=904, then choose "Plot diagram" to start the interactive Freytag's pyramid generator.

- For complicated novels or short stories, students often find it helpful to compare their group's work with that of another to ensure they have not missed key elements of the plot. It is at this time that they might also see that additional features need to be added to their graphic to fully convey their interpretations of a text.

INTO THE CLASSROOM

Fourth Grade—Realistic Fiction

THIS CLASSROOM EXAMPLE ADDRESSES THIS STANDARD

CCSS.ELA-Literacy.RL.4.7.

Make connections between the text of a story or drama and a visual or oral presentation of the text, identifying where each version reflects specific descriptions and directions in the text.

Determining the Need

Mr. Maalouf's fourth graders studied realistic fiction, and some students had chosen *Hoot* (Hiaasen, 2002) as their literature circles selection. *Hoot* has a Lexile of 760, an appropriate level for many fourth graders. The structure of the story is an important consideration as students learn to work with elements of literature, such as plot, and read longer, more complex novels. Mr. Maalouf knew from overhearing his students' informal conversations with peers that they liked to compare the book with the cinematic version. He decided to harness the power of this text-to-text interest by having each literature circle group examine a novel for which there is a movie version. And he had just the graphic organizer to help with the task.

Introducing It

Mr. Maalouf began reciting a list of well-known titles: "*Bridge To Terabithia, Because of Winn Dixie, Hoot, Charlotte's Web, Charlie and the Chocolate Factory, Harry Potter* . . . class, where am I going with this list?" Lots of hands waved enthusiastically. They'd gotten it. Books with movie versions. He asked if they preferred to read a book and then watch the movie, or the other way around. Most students said they like to watch the movie first, and several mentioned that the movie had inspired them to read the book. They explored reasons why the movies might be different than the text version, and Mr. Maalouf recorded their ideas on the whiteboard. His fourth graders were pretty astute about how the film medium imposed certain constraints on conveying the plot of the book, and on the other hand opened up possibilities for conveying meaning not possible on the book page.

Mr. Maalouf displayed Freytag's pyramid on the whiteboard and said it would help students compare plot structures. To do it well, they would need to ascertain the key elements of the storyline in each version. The example he showed was for a novel they had all read the previous month, with the main points filled in.

At the end of the discussion, he said they would complete an organizer on their own after reading their novel and seeing the movie. Then they would come together as a class to compare the differences, and the similarities, between the two art forms and see if they could come to a consensus about them.

Guided and Independent Practice

Once students completed the reading, each literature circle group sat down with chart paper and drew a pyramid like the one shown in Figure 4-4 on page 53. The chart paper allowed them to work collaboratively on a large piece of paper so that each student could grab a marker and add their thoughts. Mr. Maalouf walked around as students worked, asking them questions about their work and listening to their discussions. When it seemed appropriate, he pointed out areas where students might have neglected a key event in the movie and novel versions of the stories. The *Hoot* group noticed that they needed to focus on the conflict between the group of kids who were trying to save the burrowing owl colony and the corporation that wanted to build on the owls' nesting habitat. Mr. Maalouf praised them for connecting two key elements of literature, plot and conflict, as a means of comparing the book and the movie.

Closure

Students continued to create Freytag's pyramids for the book and the movie. Next, they noted what was different and drew some conclusions as to why those differences occurred based on the presentation media, book, or movie. Each group met with two other groups to share their findings. Finally, each student wrote a brief review of the book and movie, including a summarization of each based on the two Freytag's pyramid organizers they had constructed with their groups.

Reading, Writing, and Discussion Extensions

The power of a well-written or well-told narrative, especially as fiction, is part of the psyche of every human (see Olson, 1968). Freytag's pyramid gives students multiple opportunities to discuss a story during or after reading based on the plot and to refer to the pyramid for future written or multimodal compositions as well. Additional interactive graphic organizers your students may like can be found on the ReadWriteThink website: www.readwritethink.org/files/resources/interactives/storymap.

Students Create Their Own

After they consider these various graphic organizers, invite students to design a graphic they think could be used when reading or writing fiction. Be sure to have them explain their thinking. We encourage you to take every opportunity to move students toward crafting their personal graphic organizers.

GRAPHIC ORGANIZERS SUPPORT INFORMATIONAL TEXT READING AND WRITING TASKS

Informational texts are referred to in a variety of ways. They may be characterized as nonfiction or as expository text, for example. They may develop an argument, report observations, explain a process (how-to), or advance a persuasive perspective (even though that term is not included in the Common Core State Standards, it's a useful term students "get"). However one characterizes informational text, graphic organizers help students understand the genre as they read and organize information to determine the author's purpose, or as they create a graphic to present their own written or multimodal compositions. The examples in this chapter support these purposes.

TEXT SEARCH AND FIND BOARD

Contributed by Rebecca Kavel

THIS ORGANIZER ADDRESSES THESE STANDARDS

CCSS.ELA-Literacy.CCRA.R.3.

Analyze how and why individuals, events, or ideas develop and interact over the course of a text.

CCSS.ELA-Literacy.CCRA.R.4.

Interpret words and phrases as they are used in a text, including determining technical, connotative, and figurative meanings, and analyze how specific word choices shape meaning or tone.

What Is a Text Search and Find Board?

FIGURE 5-1
Text Search
and Find Board

Title	Main Idea	Key Details	Vocabulary
Include the book title and your name here.	*What's the main idea? Write a complete sentence that tells the main idea.*	*Provide at least three key facts that support your main idea.*	*List and define at least three important vocabulary words from the book.*
Connections	**Chart, Illustration, or Graph**	**Questions**	**Answers**
How does this text remind you of something in your life or another text you have read?	*Create a chart, illustration, or graph to display some of the information you learned from the book.*	*After reading your book, create questions.*	*Choose at least one of your questions and provide an answer with supporting details from the text.*

Source: Created by Rebecca Kavel.

Adapted from Laura Candler's (2012) informational text sharing boards, a text search and find board (Figure 5-1) allows students to determine the main idea, explain events or procedures, and determine the meaning of selected vocabulary. As students answer questions and pose them using the informational text as their source, they are pushed to think more deeply about each word and the relationship among the words. When answering the questions, students cite evidence offering written interpretation of a text while using relevant evidence to support their points and the main idea.

Comprehension improves when teachers give explicit instruction in the use of comprehension strategies (Duke & Pearson, 2002). When using this graphic organizer, students are prompted to think about what they read and record their thoughts. The board allows students to engage as active readers by analyzing and organizing important information and identifying key details. The text search and find board can be used with a variety of genres and subject areas but fits particularly well with social studies and science curricula as students articulate their knowledge stating the main idea, providing supporting details, and using higher order thinking skills to craft questions about their reading. Students can, without significant scaffolding, comprehend and evaluate complex texts across a range of disciplines. This graphic organizer helps students build strong content knowledge needed for successful reading skills using informational text.

How Do I Use a Text Search and Find Board?

- Model how to complete the board. Share that it is a great tool for students to use during and after reading.
- Explain to students that they will work independently or with a partner to complete at least three boxes. (You may adjust the number of boxes students must complete in one class period as this may take more than 2 days to complete, depending on the length of the text.)
- Review the expectations for each section.
- Give each student a text search and find board to complete, or allow students to use construction paper to create their own by folding the paper in half "hot dog" style or lengthwise and then fold it over three times to create a square and then unfold to have eight boxes.

INTO THE CLASSROOM

Third/Fourth Grade—Astronomy

CCSS.ELA-Literacy.RI.3.1.
Ask and answer questions to demonstrate understanding of a text, referring explicitly to the text as a basis.

CCSS.ELA-Literacy.RI.3.2.
Determine the main idea of a text; recount the key details and explain how they support the main idea.

CCSS.ELA-Literacy.RI.4.2.
Determine the main idea of a text and explain how it is supported by key details; summarize the text.

CCSS.ELA-Literacy.RI.4.3.
Explain events, procedures, ideas, or concepts in a historical, scientific or technical text, including what happened and why, based on specific information in a text.

CCSS.ELA-Literacy.RI.4.4.
Determine the meaning of general academic and domain-specific words or phrases in a text relevant to grade 4 topic or subject areas.

THIS CLASSROOM EXAMPLE ADDRESSES THESE STANDARDS

Determining the Need

Everything about space intrigued Ms. Kavel's third and fourth graders. They had just watched the Perseid meteor shower with their parents for homework, and they were eager to learn more. Ms. Kavel knew that using the text search and find board would help her students identify and record main ideas and key findings as they read a selection about astronomy and space in their science textbook.

After reading a section in their astronomy textbook, students watched as Ms. Kavel modeled how to fill in the graphic organizer, which she had projected onto a whiteboard. Using the directions for the text search and find (Figure 5-2), she showed them how to complete the board, enlisting class responses to complete one or two selected boxes.

Guided and Independent Practice

After giving directions for completion (this may take more than one class period), Ms. Kavel had students work independently or with a partner using the text search and find board to identify the main idea of the text, record key details and vocabulary words, and create questions and answers using higher level thinking stems (see Figure 5-3 for a student example).

Closure

After the board is completed, students use their findings to write a summary of the selected text. Teachers may use a blank template or have students create their own board out of construction paper for future lessons. We encourage you to always support students' independent crafting of graphic organizers because doing so promotes their attempts to share their thinking through a visual they feel best represents their interpretations and initiation of ideas.

FIGURE 5-2
Directions for Using a Text Search and Find Board

Title	**Main Idea**	**Key Details**	**Vocabulary**
Include the book title and your name here. *Remember to write neatly and include the date.*	*What's the main idea? Write a complete sentence that tells the main idea.* *Remember that the main idea is only one sentence long. You will have the opportunity to provide a summary at the end.*	*Provide at least three key facts that support your main idea.* *Use the text to find answers. Be sure to use the charts and illustrations the author provides.*	*List and define at least three important vocabulary words from the book.* *Choose words that are unfamiliar. If it is applicable, please include a small sketch.*
Connections	**Chart, Illustration, or Graph**	**Questions**	**Answers**
How does this text remind you of something in your life or another text you have read? *Remember to think about the news, TV shows, books, and experiences.*	*Create a chart, illustration, or graph to display some of the information you learned from the book.* *You may use the back of this paper for this activity.*	*After reading your book, create four questions.* *(Note to teacher: Based on the level of your students, you may want to require students to use higher-level thinking stems such as Marzano's or Bloom's questioning.)*	*Choose at least two of your questions and provide answers with supporting details from the text.* *If you are working with a partner, you may trade questions for this portion of the lesson.*

Source: Created by Rebecca Kavel, adapted from Laura Candler's (2012) Informational Text Sharing Board.

FIGURE 5-3
Student Example of a
Text Search and Find
Board

Title	Main Idea	Key Details	Vocabulary
Astronomy and Space	This selected text provides examples of how astronomers find out about the universe and special equipment they use.	Astronomers use optical telescopes, radio telescopes, space stations, and space probes to learn about the universe.	Asteroid: large chunks of rock or rock and metal formed with the Solar System about 5,000 million years ago.
Completed by: (student name)		Space is too dark and far away to just use a telescope so astronomers need a lot of special equipment.	Optical telescope: uses light to magnify objects to look into deep space.
			Space probe: tools with cameras sent to investigate deep space and transmit findings back to Earth.

Connections	Chart, Illustration, or Graph	Questions	Answers
This book reminds me of the museum I went to in Washington, DC, with my family. We got to sit in a real rocket.	Saturn	1. What would happen if astronomers did not have access to technology?	1. Astronomers would not be able to see any details without technology.
		2. What are the cause and effect of meteoroids falling into Earth's atmosphere?	2. When meteoroids fall into Earth's atmosphere they burn up and make a bright streak across the sky. When they fall they are called meteors.
		3. What is the biggest telescope astronomers use?	3. The largest radio telescope is the Arecibo dish in Puerto Rico. It is 305m wide. See pages 9 and 10.
		4. What are the differences in size between the Sun and the Earth?	4. The diameter of the Sun is about 1,390,000 kilometers. The diameter of the Earth is 12,742 kilometers or about 109 times smaller than the Sun.

Reading, Writing, and Discussion Extensions

As students read the assigned or self-selected text, they engage with specific purposes in mind that include thinking about and expressing new questions that arise from the reading. Based on what students learn from their reading, they might also create a written or multimodal product that supports learning even more and sharing through presentation or discussion with classmates, parents, or the world via the Internet. Consider in what ways their thinking might have similarities with the I-chart and I-guide presented later in this book.

4-SQUARE WITH A DIAMOND

Contributed by Jennifer Harahus

THIS ORGANIZER ADDRESSES THIS STANDARD **CCSS.ELA-Literacy.CCRA.W.2.**

Write informative/explanatory texts to examine and convey complex ideas and information clearly and accurately through the effective selection, organization, and analysis of content.

What Is 4-Square With a Diamond?

FIGURE 5-4
4-Square With a Diamond

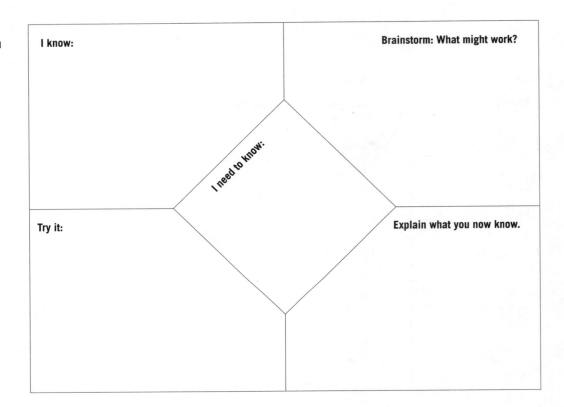

A 4-square with a diamond organizer helps scaffold learners' understanding of the steps in a process, helping learners explain them verbally or in writing. In answering questions on the organizer, they are led into analytical thinking. Students might also use the organizer to show and explain each step in a process. Students are graded using a rubric (see the example in Figure 5-4) that evaluates knowledge, approaches or strategies used, and explanation of the learning (Zollman, 2009).

For example, in science, the graphic organizer can be used during hands-on investigations. Students would be presented with the investigation/lab procedures and as they worked through the steps, the 4-square would serve as a record of attempted processes. In this way, they use the organizer as a framework for listening as directions are given. This organizer could also support the inquiry model as students must decide on the possible processes and record results of each attempt.

How Do I Use a 4-Square With a Diamond?

- Choose a situation or problem central to your objective.
- Model thinking through a similar problem.
- Model answering questions and writing in the graphic organizer.
- Share the rubric with students.
- Give the 4-square and a new problem to students to work through.

INTO THE CLASSROOM

Fourth Grade—Math

CCSS.ELA-Literacy.L.4.1a.
Use relative pronouns (who, whose, whom, which, that) and relative adverbs (where, when, why).

CCSS.ELA-Literacy.L.4.4a.
Use context (e.g., definitions, examples, or restatements in text) as a clue to the meaning of a word or phrase.

CCSS.ELA-Literacy.RF.4.4a.
Read grade-level text with purpose and understanding.

THIS CLASSROOM EXAMPLE ADDRESSES THESE STANDARDS

Determining the Need

Ms. Harahus showed students how to use the 4-square with a diamond graphic organizer and was heartened to see that many students immediately found it would help them systematically work through a word problem by considering prior knowledge, what needs to be found, ways to solve the problem, and explanations to aid in the written response. She liked that the organizer would also give her a concrete, more complete view of her students' thinking as they worked through a problem.

Introducing It

Here is a word problem Ms. Harahus gave students as they practiced using the organizer: "You are reading a book with 153 pages. If you want to read the same number of pages each night, how many would you have to read each night to finish in 10 days?"

Next, she asked students to consider the following word problem while completing the organizer on their own: "Julia cut a string 8.43 m long into 6 equal pieces. What is the length of each piece of string?"

Guided and Independent Practice

As students worked through the word problem using the organizer, Ms. Harahus asked them to write the information given in the problem in the first section and what they need to find out in the center. She then helped them think about different ways to solve the problem. (The teacher should model for the students how to reword the problem and record a variety of problem-solving methods.) This encouraged students' independent crafting of visuals that represented their thinking.

After completing the problem, students explained the answer in a reflection. Ms. Harahus assessed their work using the rubric in Figure 5-5. An example of student work is shown in Figure 5-6.

FIGURE 5-5
Rubric for 4-Square
With a Diamond

Score	Knowledge	Strategy	Explanation
4	All of the work was correct.	Student created a plan and followed through with the plan.	Student's explanation was detailed and included all information.
3	Most of the work was correct.	Student's plan was incomplete but a plan was chosen and used.	Student's explanation included most of the information.
2	Some of the work was correct.	Student's plan and process did not match.	Student's explanation lacked detail.
1	Little of the work was correct.	Student's plan was largely incomplete.	Student's explanation had major gaps.
0	Student did not attempt.	Student did not plan.	Student did not explain.

FIGURE 5-6

Example of Student Response Using 4-Square With a Diamond

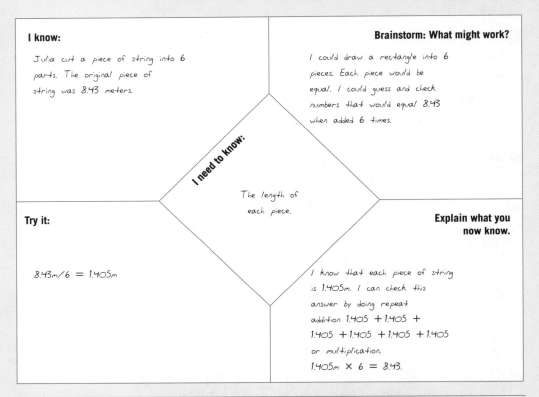

Source: Contributed by Jennifer Harahus.

Reading, Writing, and Discussion Extensions

After students complete their own versions of the 4-square with a diamond, ask them to work with a partner or small group to compare their work through discussion. What did each student contribute? What did students add to their 4-square with a diamond organizers after discussion? You may also ask students to write or explain their thinking processes as they used the 4-square with a diamond approach to a new word problem. This organizer is useful when instructional tasks require students to apply background knowledge, define the problem, identify what they may not know, and then make an attempt at resolution.

MODIFIED KWL

CCSS.ELA-Literacy.CCRA.R.2.

Determine central ideas or themes of a text and analyze their development; summarize the key supporting details and ideas.

CCSS.ELA-Literacy.CCRA.R.3.

Analyze how and why individuals, events, or ideas develop and interact over the course of a text.

CCSS.ELA-Literacy.CCRA.R.10.

Read and comprehend complex literary and informational texts independently and proficiently.

THIS ORGANIZER ADDRESSES THESE STANDARDS

What Is a Modified KWL?

K What do we know about the KWL instructional strategy?	W What do we want to know about the KWL instructional strategy?	L What did we learn about the KWL instructional strategy?
Categories:		

FIGURE 5-7
KWL

One of the most widely recognized instructional routines is KWL (know, want to know, learn; Ogle, 1986). There are more than a dozen published variations on the elegant theme captured in this approach. A challenge teachers face with this approach is that what students want to know is somewhat uninformed because they simply lack sophisticated knowledge of the topic that could lead toward increasingly deep connections to the content. Adapting the approach to feature discipline-specific texts may help (Gillis, 2014). You may have noticed a section at the bottom of the KWL chart in Figure 5-7 for "Categories." This part is often left off, but it should not be. After brainstorming in column one what they already know about the topic, students are asked to categorize the information they have brainstormed. Doing so is what Ogle (1986) calls "content-structuring" (p. 566) and helps students create cognitive maps of the material they already know.

One adaptation of KWL is intended to support students as they propose questions about problems they encounter in mathematics. In KWC (Hyde, 2006), students identify in the first column "What do you know for sure?" In the second column, they identify "What are you trying to find out?" In the third column, they decide, "Are there special conditions or precise words to address?" A space underneath asks students to show how they solve the problem using pictures, numbers, and words (see Figure 5-8).

What do you know for sure?	What are you trying to find out?	Are there special conditions or precise words to address?
Solution:		

FIGURE 5-8
Using What I Know to Solve a Problem

Example: Social Studies

Critical to understanding history is the capacity to handle dissonance or noise (Vansledright, 2012) between and among accounts of the events that constitute the historical record. Who actors (i.e., the historical individuals who did things) are and their purposes for creating an account are important details to historians. KWL can be easily modified to increase understanding of history as a discipline. Source documents, readily available via the Internet, provide differing views and accounts of social phenomena. By adding rows for each document examined (which could include a textbook), the familiar pattern of know–want/need to know–learned becomes a scaffold to assist students as they begin their thinking work with multiple documents (see Figure 5-9).

FIGURE 5-9
KWL Adapted for Analysis of Multiple Historical Accounts

	What I know about the document before reading:	What I need to learn as I read:	What I learned about this document and its author:
Document A			
Document B			
Document C			
Synthesis and conclusions:			

Example: Science

Scientists often work back and forth between alphabetic texts and the graphs, charts, and other images that accompany and expand on these texts (Shanahan & Shanahan, 2008). KWL is, once again, easily modified to develop the ways struggling readers and readers learning English as a second language make sense of discipline-specific texts in science. In this example, students work with a single text and a column is added to highlight the role of graphics in the text (see Figure 5-10).

FIGURE 5-10
KWL for Science Texts With Graphics

Text and page or chapter numbers:			
What I know about this topic:	What I need to know about it:	What I learned from the written text:	What I learned from the graphics or data:
Categories:		Synthesis of text and graphics/data:	

How Do I Use a KWL?

- Decide what the features of the text might be that are particular to the discipline (e.g., science, social studies).
- Adapt the KWL chart to emphasize those text features.

- Choose texts that challenge readers but don't overwhelm them. Often, more than one text might be helpful at several levels of difficulty.
- Make copies of the KWL chart, share it digitally, or help students construct their own.
- Ask students to read the text and use the KWL chart to guide their thinking.
- In small groups, or with the whole class, use the students' individually created and modified KWL charts to discuss the standards-based concept that is characterized in the text.

INTO THE CLASSROOM

Fifth Grade—Ecosystems

CCSS.ELA-Literacy.RI.5.2.

Determine two or more main ideas of a text and explain how they are supported by key details; summarize the text.

CCSS.ELA-Literacy.RI.5.9.

Integrate information from several texts on the same topic in order to write or speak about the subject knowledgeably.

THIS CLASSROOM EXAMPLE ADDRESSES THESE STANDARDS

Determining the Need

Mrs. Collier wanted her fifth-grade students to understand the principle of how an animal census was taken as they worked to understand how ecosystems represent the interactions of many different species. A recent census of great white sharks off the central California coast provided her with the opportunity she needed. An article she read in the newspaper turned out to have a Lexile rating of 1490 (Sahagun, 2013). Falling in the Grade 11 band, this text was much too difficult for most of her students. She searched the web and found a challenging *Scholastic* article (Modigliani, 2011) written for student audiences. Although the Lexile rating for this text fell in the Grade 6–8 band for complexity, its visuals made it a much more manageable challenge for her students. The *Scholastic* article also included a video, so Mrs. Collier decided to adapt a KWL for science reading.

Introducing It

Counting animals in the wild, especially at sea, seemed to be a simple enough task at first. Mrs. Collier showed students a video of a school of fish swimming in a large aquarium. She used the search term "aquarium school of fish" and clicked the video search button to find many examples, but she chose just one. Next, she asked students to count the fish, a task they found very difficult because the fish kept moving and it was hard to keep track of which ones they had counted and which ones had moved to another part of the tank.

Students logged onto their iPads and found the *Scholastic* article, which Mrs. Collier had linked on her class web page. Next, she asked students to use the graphic organizer format. Instead of making a copy for students, she asked them to use a ruler to quickly mark the long side of a paper about every two inches—best guesses would be fine, she told them. The goal was to have five columns. She then had students fold off the bottom third of the paper. At the top of each column, Mrs. Collier asked students to write in the headings in Figure 5-11, which she had also written on the board.

FIGURE 5-11
What Mrs. Collier Wrote
on the Board

What I know about this topic:	What I need to know about it:	What I learned from the written text:	What I learned from the video and pictures:	What I still need to know:

Note: See **www.corwin.com/miningcomplextext/2-5** for video instructions.

Some students wanted to know if they could write sideways in the column, and Mrs. Collier told them they could. She then reminded them of the objective for the lesson: How do scientists create a census of wildlife when the animals move and often hide from humans?

Guided and Independent Practice

Notice that the heading in the fourth column of Figure 5-11 is changed from the traditional KWL format to reflect the literacy demands of the selected text, and a fifth column was also added. Mrs. Collier challenged her young readers to question the text more thoroughly in order to fill in the last column. The *Scholastic* article told them much that they needed to know about why sharks, scary as they are, are also important. What that article did not tell them was how a census of animals was taken. To answer that, students—now armed with some basic information—needed to read the more complex article in the newspaper or find an alternative source and craft graphic organizers to illustrate similarities and differences across the texts.

Closure

Students collaboratively shared their findings with the class and began the next phase of their inquiry to learn how other wildlife censuses are taken and why humans need to know how many different types of animals there are. Figure 5-12 shows a student example.

FIGURE 5-12
Student Example of a Modified KWL That Reflects Scientific Thinking

Text and page or chapter numbers:				
What I know about this topic:	**What I need to know about it:**	**What I learned from the written text:**	**What I learned from the video and pictures:**	**What I still need to know:**
Sharks are scary and sometimes eat people. Not all sharks are scary. Some sharks might help everyone.	Why sharks might be important to people or other animals. How do scientists know how many sharks there are?	Some people slice off shark fins for food and throw away the shark. Sharks help keep the populations of other fish from becoming too large.	Shark attacks don't happen often. Sometimes sharks attack people because they look like seals, a favorite food. Sharks have big teeth. The whale shark is as big as a bus.	How do scientists actually know how many sharks there are under all that water?

Categories: Describe sharks Benefits of sharks Danger from sharks Counting sharks	**Synthesis of text, video, and pictures:** Even though sharks seem scary, they are helpful in the environment and to humans, too. Scientists have a big challenge to count the number of sharks in the ocean.

Reading, Writing, and Discussion Extensions

KWL is predicated on the idea that engaged learners want to know more about the world and the texts they encounter there. What other graphic organizers in this book, and elsewhere, encourage students to engage with text in a way that leads them to want to know more than they currently do? Why do you think so?

When students recognize that they know some things, but they need or want to know more, they tend to want to read to find out what they do not know. They tend toward writing and other expressive communications to share what they have learned, and they want to talk about the ideas they have found and the new questions that have presented themselves as they investigate their learning.

TABBED BOOK MANIPULATIVE

Contributed by Kim Heintschel Ramadan

CCSS.ELA-Literacy.CCRA.R.1.

Read closely to determine what the text says explicitly and to make logical inferences from it; cite specific textual evidence when writing or speaking to support conclusions drawn from the text.

CCSS.ELA-Literacy.CCRA.R.5.

Analyze the structure of texts, including how specific sentences, paragraphs, and larger portions of the text (e.g., a section, chapter, scene, or stanza) relate to each other and the whole.

CCSS.ELA-Literacy.CCRA.W.4.

Produce clear and coherent writing in which the development, organization, and style are appropriate to task, purpose, and audience.

What Is a Tabbed Book Manipulative?

FIGURE 5-13
Tabbed Book Manipulative

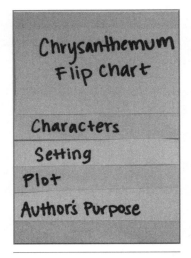

Source: Contributed by Kim Heintschel Ramadan, Teacher Leader and Doctoral Student at UNCC.

FIGURE 5-14
Organization of Tabs for a Science Topic

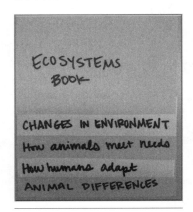

Source: Contributed by Kim Heintschel Ramadan, Teacher Leader and Doctoral Student at UNCC.

The manipulative strategy guide is a foldable graphic organizer (Wood, Lapp, Flood, & Taylor, 2008). This type of manipulative guide is described as a "3D, student made, interactive graphic organizer" (Zike, n.d., p. 1). A tabbed book is a version of a foldable guide that can be used to create any sort of book (see Figure 5-13). It can be used to create books or as graphic organizers to display information. It is easy to manipulate because of the tabbed edges.

Example: Science

Fourth-grade curriculum typically calls for students to study environmental changes. Students could use a tabbed book to demonstrate their understanding of the changes, adaptation, and behaviors in an ecosystem (see Figure 5-14). On the first tab, students could give examples of beneficial and harmful changes to an organism's environment. On the second tab, students could explain how animals meet their need by changing their behavior in response to their environment. On the third tab, students could explain how humans adapt to their environment. Finally, on the fourth tab students could explain how animals differ in the same population.

How Do My Students Create a Tabbed Book?

1. Collect several pieces of 8½ × 11 paper. We have noticed that students seem to like colored copy paper for activities such as this.

2. Fold the stack in half lengthwise.

3. Staple together to form a book.

4. Starting with the front of the book, cut overlapping pieces so a tab is left on each page.

Summarizing

Summarizing is often thought of as a low-level skill; however, students who can summarize demonstrate a grasp of a text or lecture that provides a substantive foundation for moving forward with other content. In actuality, summarizing is a complex skill that requires students to attend to the important ideas in any given text (including texts to which students listen, such as an audiobook or lecture), analyze that text, and select the most relevant information as it pertains to the text itself (Marzano, Pickering, & Pollock, 2001). We avoid the use of "not important" since well-written texts often include details that are important but do not appear in a well-constructed summary. In this book, we differentiate summarization from synthesis in this way: Summarization is a task that asks students to concisely conceptualize a single text, whereas synthesis requires students to concisely conceptualize the ideas from a multiplicity of texts.

INTO THE CLASSROOM

Third Grade—Reading

CCSS.ELA-Literacy.RL.3.9.

Compare and contrast the themes, settings, and plots of stories written by the same author about the same or similar characters (e.g., in books from a series).

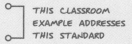 THIS CLASSROOM EXAMPLE ADDRESSES THIS STANDARD

Determining the Need

Mr. Smith is a third-grade teacher who wanted his students to have a space for responding to texts in preparation for their book club discussions during their series book club unit. One of the standards for students at the end of third grade is to compare and contrast themes, setting, and plots written by the same author. He decided his students could use a tabbed book to record their thoughts to help drive the book club discussions.

Introducing It

Mr. Smith showed a sample of this manipulative guide to the class that a former student had created; he also shared one that he had completed, based on his own reading of series books. He explained to students how to create the tabbed book and provided a list (students could also brainstorm a list) of books in the series that might appear on the tabs.

FIGURE 5-15
Student Example of
a Tabbed Book
Manipulative

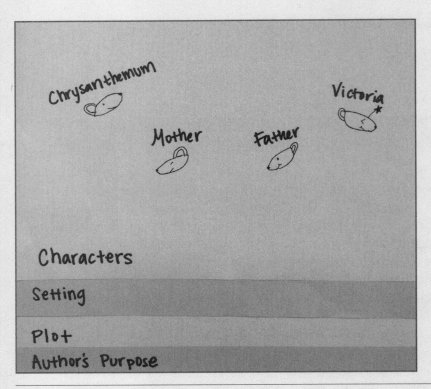

Source: Contributed by Kim Heintschel Ramadan, Teacher Leader and Doctoral Student at UNCC.

Guided or Independent Practice

As each student read a book in the series, she or he recorded the book title on the tab and wrote about the book on the page for that book (see Figure 5-15). Each tab was designated for a different book title, and the final tab was for comparisons across texts. Students could address general plot summaries, characterization, or themes on each tab.

Closure

After students created their tabbed books, Mr. Smith asked them to write a synthesis showing how the characters (or other element of literature) developed across the series. He assessed student progress toward the standard and provided feedback to students to assist them in moving forward.

Reading, Writing, and Discussion Extensions

Mr. Smith used tabbed book manipulative guides as a tool for informing discussions and a reference students could use as they talked about the different books in a series they read. Students should be encouraged to design their next books to accommodate the information they plan to present. To do so they need to consider the information being presented and then how to label the tabs to best share this information. Tabbed books have a variety of uses as a note-making tool and as a way of thinking about what students read or guiding their future writing. The examples for the tabbed book focus on literary structures (characters, theme, and so on) and science; in what ways might the tabbed book address other ways of thinking in math, social science, physical education, and other content areas that require students to read, write, discuss, or present in multimodal formats?

6

GRAPHIC ORGANIZERS SUPPORT STUDENTS' READING PROFICIENCIES

As teachers and students grapple with the staircase of text complexity (Common Core State Standards Initiative, 2010a; Wolsey, Grisham, & Heibert, 2012), the demand that students work with increasingly complex texts means that teachers must show students how to work with texts that often challenge them. The graphic organizers in this chapter, thoughtfully used, can assist students to make sense of texts that may seem difficult at first.

SOMEBODY-WANTED-BUT-SO

Contributed by Brian Williams

CCSS.ELA-Literacy.CCRA.R.2.

Determine central ideas or themes of a text and analyze their development; summarize the key supporting details and ideas.

What Is Somebody-Wanted-But-So?

FIGURE 6-1
Somebody-Wanted-But-So

Somebody (Characters)	
Wanted (Plot motivation)	
But (Conflict)	
So (Resolution)	

The somebody-wanted-but-so (Macon, Bewell, & Vogt, 1991) graphic organizer (Figure 6-1) is a simple template that allows students to succinctly summarize a lengthy piece of literature in one or two sentences. The central ideas of the text are highlighted as the template uses the words *somebody, wanted, but,* and *so* to guide students in processing the important parts of the literature. Each key word prompts students to recognize specific aspects of a given story. *Somebody* recognizes the characters, *wanted* highlights the plot motivation, *but* illuminates the conflict, and *so* states the resolution of the story. In addition, key words are used to successfully aid students in focusing on the chronological development of the story. This graphic organizer can be used in any content area and with nonfiction texts.

How Do I Use Somebody-Wanted-But-So?

- Review the literary terms *characters, plot motivation, conflict,* and *resolution.*
- Read aloud to students or have them read in groups or independently a short story.
- On large chart paper, on the board, or on a digitally projected version, model to students your thinking while filling out the somebody-wanted-but-so graphic organizer (Figure 6-2).
- Model converting the completed graphic organizer into a one- or two-sentence summary (Figure 6-2).
- Give students a new short story and template.
- Allow students to complete the new template in groups of two.
- Review answers to the new template.
- Instruct students to read the lesson's main text, and allow them to complete the graphic organizer independently.

Somebody (Characters)	Hermione
Wanted (Plot motivation)	Acceptance as a respected student at Hogwarts School of Witchcraft and Wizardry
But (Conflict)	Those who resented her Muggle ancestry constantly thwarted her efforts.
So (Resolution)	She worked twice as hard to be better than everyone else in her studies.

FIGURE 6-2
Somebody-Wanted-But-So Using *Harry Potter and the Sorcerer's Stone*

Summary Sentence

In J. K. Rowling's *Harry Potter and the Sorcerer's Stone*, Hermione **wanted** to be accepted as a respected student at Hogwarts School of Witchcraft and Wizardry, **but** those who resented her Muggle ancestry constantly thwarted her efforts, **so** she worked twice as hard to be better than everyone else in her studies at school.

Content Area Examples

Even though somebody-wanted-but-so works well with narrative fiction, it is useful in other content areas where a story or narrative is part of the reading tasks. Math and history are good examples.

Math

Word problems in story format are a type of text that often befuddles students. By using the somebody-wanted-but-so format, students can break down a word problem in a manner that is comprehensible to them (see Figure 6-3).

Somebody (Characters)	John
Wanted (Plot motivation)	$20 to attend the upcoming theatrical performance
But (Conflict)	He did not have any money.
So (Resolution)	He cut 2 lawns at $10 each, totaling the needed $20 to attend the show.

FIGURE 6-3
Somebody-Wanted-But-So Math Example

Summary Sentence

John **wanted** $20 to attend the upcoming theatrical performance, **but** he did not have any money, **so** he cut 2 lawns at $10 each, totaling the needed $20 to attend the show.

History

History texts are filled with stories. To summarize a historical even through the eyes of *somebody*, students may use somebody-wanted-but-so to get at the essence of the event.

Students who have just read a text about Abraham Lincoln and the problems associated with putting an end to slavery might construct an organizer like the one in Figure 6-4.

FIGURE 6-4
Somebody-Wanted-
But-So History Example

Somebody (Characters)	Abraham Lincoln
Wanted (Plot motivation)	To end slavery
But (Conflict)	He knew that ending slavery was limited by the Constitution.
So (Resolution)	He created and signed the Emancipation Proclamation to free slaves in 10 states not under Union control.

Summary Sentence

Abraham Lincoln **wanted** to end slavery, **but** he knew that ending slavery was limited by the Constitution, **so** he created and signed the Emancipation Proclamation to free slaves in 10 states not yet under Union control.

INTO THE CLASSROOM

Second Grade—Retelling/Summarizing

THIS CLASSROOM
EXAMPLE ADDRESSES
THIS STANDARD

CCSS.ELA-Literacy.RL.1.9.

Compare and contrast the adventures and experiences of characters in stories.

Determining the Need

In Mr. Abramovich's second-grade classroom, students were learning that stories had a structure they could summarize or retell. Students told him what they knew about caterpillars and any they had seen. Most knew that caterpillars could become butterflies.

Introducing It

On the digital projector, Mr. Abramovich displayed the organizer shown in Figure 6-1. Next, he told students they would read a book about a caterpillar named Charlie who could not find any friends (Deluise, 1990). He pointed out that they would need to listen carefully as he read aloud to decide who the characters were, what they wanted, what was difficult, and how things turned out. The students always loved read-aloud time, and they listened carefully.

Guided and Independent Practice

After reading the story aloud, Mr. Abramovich gave each group a copy of the organizer he had displayed and a copy of the book *Charlie, the Caterpillar* by Dom Deluise. The students read the story for themselves, and then they filled in the somebody-wanted-but-so organizer. Most groups came up with an organizer that looked like the one in Figure 6-5.

Somebody	Charlie, the caterpillar
Wanted	Some friends
But	Most of the other animals thought he was ugly.
So	Charlie became a butterfly and made friends with a caterpillar who would be a butterfly someday.

FIGURE 6-5
Somebody-Wanted-But-So Using *Charlie, the Caterpillar*

Closure

After each group read aloud their somebody-wanted-but-so statements, Mr. Abramovich pointed out that what they had just learned to do was summarize a story. He asked students to name a few books they had read during the last week or two, and students brainstormed a list. Then each student chose a favorite story and created a somebody-wanted-but-so organizer for it. Mr. Abramovich circulated through the room as students worked, and he kept careful notes about who might need additional help or practice with this summarizing task.

Reading, Writing, and Discussion Extensions

Students were invited to compare their somebody-wanted-but-so summaries with others to note similarities or differences that identified key components of the text. Often, in writing, students must summarize narrative sources, and this organizer helps them think through the summary process in a succinct way. Many of the graphic organizers in this book ask students to summarize a source in some way or synthesize multiple sources.

Students Create Their Own

Invite students to think about which organizer is the best fit for the summary task they are being asked to complete. Also, always encourage them to craft their own graphic if they feel those available aren't really supportive of their thinking.

UNDERSTANDING TEXT STRUCTURES: FIVE TEXT TYPES

These text types cut across many Standards, including the following:

CCSS.ELA-Literacy.CCRA.R.5.

Analyze the structure of texts, including how specific sentences, paragraphs, and larger portions of the text (e.g., a section, chapter, scene, or stanza) relate to each other and the whole.

CCSS.ELA-Literacy.CCRA.R.8.

Delineate and evaluate the argument and specific claims in a text, including the validity of the reasoning as well as the relevance and sufficiency of the evidence.

Figure 6-6 shows the progression from Grades 1 through 5 for anchor standards R.5 and R.8.

FIGURE 6-6
Progression of Text Structure Types in the Common Core State Standards, Grades 1–5

First Grade	CCSS.ELA-Literacy.RI.1.5. Know and use various text features (e.g., headings, tables of contents, glossaries, electronic menus, icons) to locate key facts or information in a text.
	CCSS.ELA-Literacy.RI.1.8. Identify the reasons an author gives to support points in a text.
Second Grade	CCSS.ELA-Literacy.RI.2.5. Know and use various text features (e.g., captions, bold print, subheadings, glossaries, indexes, electronic menus, icons) to locate key facts or information in a text efficiently.
	CCSS.ELA-Literacy.RI.2.8. Describe how reasons support specific points the author makes in a text.
Third Grade	CCSS.ELA-Literacy.RI.3.5. Use text features and search tools (e.g., key words, sidebars, hyperlinks) to locate information relevant to a given topic efficiently.
	CCSS.ELA-Literacy.RI.3.8. Describe the logical connection between particular sentences and paragraphs in a text (e.g., comparison, cause/effect, first/second/third in a sequence).
Fourth Grade	CCSS.ELA-Literacy.RI.4.5. Describe the overall structure (e.g., chronology, comparison, cause/effect, problem/solution) of events, ideas, concepts, or information in a text or part of a text.
	CCSS.ELA-Literacy.RI.4.8. Explain how an author uses reasons and evidence to support particular points in a text.
Fifth Grade	CCSS.ELA-Literacy.RI.5.5. Compare and contrast the overall structure (e.g., chronology, comparison, cause/effect, problem/solution) of events, ideas, concepts, or information in two or more texts.
	CCSS.ELA-Literacy.RI.5.8. Explain how an author uses reasons and evidence to support particular points in a text, identifying which reasons and evidence support which point(s).

In first and second grades, students learn to attend to text features, such as headings, and to notice the reasons an author gives to support main ideas. By third grade, students begin looking specifically at top-level structures, such as comparison and sequence, as a means of making sense of text. By fourth grade, students must begin using this information to construct a mental model of how authors organize their ideas to provide reasons and evidence in support of a coherent overall composition. Of course, these ideas translate nicely to the written and multimodal compositions students will create as well.

Sequential, Descriptive, Cause/Effect, Compare and Contrast, Problem/Solution

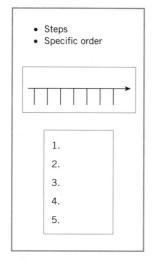

- Steps
- Specific order

1.
2.
3.
4.
5.

FIGURE 6-7 Sequential

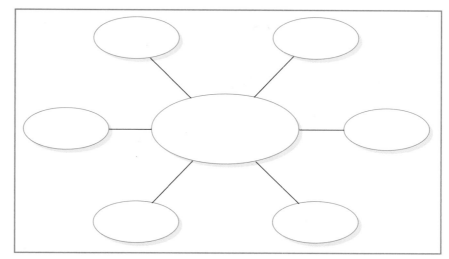

FIGURE 6-8 Descriptive

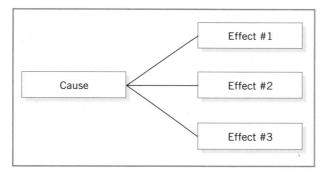

Cause

Effect #1

Effect #2

Effect #3

FIGURE 6-9 Cause/Effect

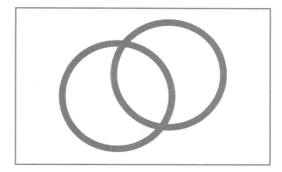

FIGURE 6-10 Compare and Contrast

What Are Text Structures?

Students sometimes struggle with top-level structures that authors use to organize their texts. Five commonly recognized text structures are sequential, descriptive, cause/effect, compare and contrast, and problem/solution (see Figures 6-7 to 6-11) (Akhondi, Malayeri, & Samad, 2011). Earlier work (Meyer, Brandt, & Bluth, 1980) suggested similar categories: stories, description, antecendent [sic]/consequent, problem/solution, and comparison (argumentative text; p. 98). Meyer et al. (1980) found that signaling could also help students identify the structure of the text; for example, when descriptive top-level structures tended to signal this pattern by using terms throughout the text similar to *for example* and *such as*.

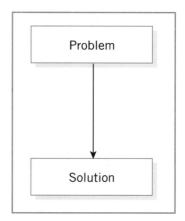

Problem

Solution

FIGURE 6-11 Problem/Solution

Top-level patterns that rely on the sequential mode may use terms such as *first, second, third, next,* and *after that.* When readers are able to recognize the top-level pattern, often when a signal indicates what the top level may be, effective readers are more able to relate concepts to that structure and attend more completely to the ideas rather than simply noting facts they encounter in a linear manner as they read.

Why are these patterns called top-level structures? Well, because few writers stick to just one pattern. Though a piece may be written as problem/solution in general, it also might include compare and contrast, descriptive, and narration, for example. Graphic organizers can help students see the top-level domains. And for complex texts, graphic organizers are flexible enough to help students attend to signal words and notice additional text structures beyond the top level. A text may begin with problem/solution as the top-level structure, but it also may include descriptive and compare-and-contrast elements, for example. Also, once students are familiar with graphic organizers for different purposes, teachers can encourage students to construct their own graphic organizers and choose the types that best fit with their purposes for writing.

Sequential

Much knowledge is organized in a sequential manner, with one event or element following another. Later in this book, we explore other common text and knowledge production patterns, but knowledge presented sequentially is worth a bit of extra time. Processes, such as how waves form or move or how archaeologists excavate a site, can be intricate. Timelines can give students a sense of historical events or some types of processes and how the elements relate to each other. Graphic organizers make it possible for students to comprehend complex processes or events through any of the language and visual arts: reading, writing, speaking, listening, visualization. Sequential organizers might include processes (think flow chart) or sequences of events (think timeline). Moreover, they have the potential to cut across standards. For that reason, this section does not list any anchor standards, but the following lessons will.

Processing is a term we encounter often when we press a submit button on a web page. But what are processes? In some ways, they differ from products, the things that result from a process. For example, we authors have a process we have evolved over the years that resulted in this book. Waves at sea are evidence of a natural process. Food is preserved following established processes. And your favorite online retailer uses specific processes to ensure that your products arrive at your door in a timely way. Mathematicians use processes or procedures, known as algorithms, for solving certain types of problems (e.g., Ives, 2007; Ives & Hoy, 2003), and your computer processes information according to a very specific, but complicated process. Some processes are straightforward while others are more complicated. Whatever the process is, if it is new or unfamiliar to students, graphic organizers can help them understand it.

Timelines are sequential organizers that permit students to understand how events unfold over time. A variety of timeline formats help students think about how events occur over fixed or regular intervals (a second, a year, a decade, and so on). Gallavan and Kottler (2010) show how timelines can help students understand patterns and positions over time. In their example, students compare the life of King Henry VIII with other events in Europe and then further compare his life with current times. Henry VIII, for instance, was born in 1491, just one year before Columbus sailed for what we now think of as the Western Hemisphere. By putting his life in the context of an event students know well (Columbus's first voyage), they can make connections and notice patterns.

When students recognize how texts are organized, the cognitive load required to determine that pattern is reduced, allowing them to focus more on what they can gather from the text and its structure. Graphic organizers can be an important tool that may help students notice that texts do, in fact, have a structure. And the more quickly they understand that structure, the more they increase the possibility of understanding what they are reading, including and going beyond that text structure (Akhondi et al., 2011).

Descriptive

"Can you describe that pizza?" he asked. "Sure," I replied, "that pizza was fantastic and the most delicious I've ever ordered. It was off the hook." As an endorsement, if you know me and what I like in pizza, this might suffice as a general description. To us, description seems to demand a bit more in academic contexts, however. Description asks readers to allow themselves to be transported outside themselves to realms about which they know little. Description allows us, when we read, to believe we are riding with Eleanor of Aquitaine on the second crusade. Description permits us to be, for a time, a professional tennis player (see Wallace, 1997) as we read about the sport. Description leads us to sense how the bread in the oven might taste just from the words alone.

Ray Bradbury, like many good authors, had a sense of description that brought his readers into the story. In *Something Wicked This Way Comes*, Bradbury (1962) does far more than say his two protagonists ran to the library. Come along with Will and Jim in Bradbury's words on their way to the local library:

> Like all boys, they never walked anywhere, but named a goal and lit for it, scissors and elbows. Nobody wanted to win. It was in their friendship they just wanted to run forever, shadow and shadow. Their hands slapped library door handles together, their chests broke track tapes together, their tennis shoes beat parallel pony tracks over lawns, trimmed bushes, squirreled trees, no one losing, both winning, thus saving friendship for another time of loss. (p. 10)

As you read Bradbury's words, you can see Will and Jim running after a question they believe they will find behind the library doors, and you feel their friendship that will carry them to the end of the story many pages later. By the time you finish the paragraph above, you probably find yourself hooked, as a reader, wanting to follow the story and the mystery in the novel. Description captures in words what our senses know intuitively. It leads readers to worlds and experiences, fictional and real, beyond their own experiences, igniting senses and emotions more specific than general.

Aristotle cautioned speakers (and we can apply the concepts to written work as well) to call things by their own special names and to avoid ambiguity (*Rhetoric*, book 3, part 5). That pizza we mentioned? If the reader or listener cannot tell the difference between the pepperoni pizza at Two Pizza Guys restaurant and the one at the Village Pizza Palace from the written description, there is little value in reading or hearing about it in the first place. What is it that makes you want that Village Pizza over the one from the Pizza Guys anyway? Graphic organizers can help the teacher who wants students to understand the role of description in works of exposition and fiction, write more effectively in either genre, speak to an audience convincingly, or understand the inner workings of the atom.

As with many things, when learners are novices with the content, processes, or culture of academic life, it is possible to overthink or tease out the parts such that the original is no longer recognizable. Graphic organizers have the power to make the parts visible, the thinking evident, the context broken into categories, but this is also a point of caution. If we pull too many threads in the beautiful tapestry, we have nothing more than a pile of colorful thread. Judicious use of graphic organizers to pry the lid from the box of description is a means toward thoughtful reading, interesting writing, and engaging speech. Some of our favorite digital tools, which represent ideas and terms visually, are in Figure 6-12.

FIGURE 6-12
Visual Representations of Words and Ideas Online

WordSift: http://wordsift.com

Visual Thesaurus: www.visualthesaurus.com

Wordflex (for iPad): http://wordflex.com

Effective description often includes some of these features, but not all of them simultaneously:

- implication on the part of the author (and the capacity for inference on the part of the reader)
- judicious use of descriptive words
- possible connection between the known and unknown
- variation and nuance of a topic that is new, underdeveloped, or specialized
- specificity relative to the concept or topic

Description lends itself well to the cluster or bubble format of graphic organizers (Olson, 1996). Clusters allow the user to expand infinitely, to work within a framework that is tightly defined, or to explore potential new connections.

Cause/Effect

Cause/effect patterns are sometimes straightforward. If we put a match next to a wadded-up newspaper, the effect is likely to be a small fire. In other instances, the cause/effect pattern is more complicated. In many ways, cause/effect text patterns are similar to the sequential and process patterns we explored earlier. Cause/effect patterns are typically thought of in terms of events: One event directly leads to and causes another. In some cases, a set of causes may lead to a single event, one cause may lead to a multiplicity of events, one event may conditionally cause another, and so on. You can infer that cause/effect text patterns are rarely as simple as they may first appear.

In addition, it is possible to mistake correlation for cause. If crime rates rise during the summer months, and ice cream sales rise during the summer, it would be incorrect to assume that ice cream consumption causes crime or vice versa. We might look for an underlying cause, however. As you can see, the opportunities to teach students to be careful thinkers about cause and effect are ample. These opportunities include explorations of science topics, historical events, political discussions, and problem/solution.

Herringbone or fishbone diagrams are useful tools for looking at cause/effect with multiple contributing variables. Refer to Figure 2-5 (page 26) for one example, though these can be quite a bit more complex.

Compare and Contrast

Compare and contrast is a common direction given to students. "Compare and contrast the articles in the *New York Times* with the *San Francisco Chronicle* on the recent visit of the president to the drought-stricken west." "Compare and contrast the models of the atom we have discussed this week." And on it goes. But just what does it mean to compare and contrast? The role of analogy is important here. As Gick and Holyoak (1983) remind us, "The analogist notes correspondences between the known problem and a new unsolved one, and on that basis derives an analogous potential solution. More generally, the function of an analogy is to derive a new solution, hypothesis, or prediction" (p. 5). An important key to comparison is that it is all about noting similarity between things. Contrast is all about noting the differences. Overarching all is that the task is not an end unto itself. We could compare and contrast the proverbial apples and oranges, but unless we can identify a purpose for doing so and the attributes that are worth studying, the exercise might be futile.

In compare-and-contrast tasks, students must look at two or more different things, be they concepts, objects, texts, and so on. Then the task becomes one of noting what is common among the items to be compared and what is relevant to the purpose of comparison in the first place. Next, the items to be compared must be contrasted to note what is different about them. The process of determining relevant similarities and distinguishing features comes down to what attributes are important. Teachers may ask students to compare and contrast the characters of Harry Potter and Hermione Granger from the Harry Potter series of books by J. K. Rowling. They may notice that Harry is a boy and Hermione is a girl. Harry has a scar on his forehead and Hermione does not. However, these features may only be superficial to the task of compare and contrast since these are obvious and do not encourage deeper examination of the characters or the text in which they appear. For a useful interactive tool for thinking about compare-and-contrast structures, go to www.readwritethink.org/files/resources/interactives/compcontrast.

Venn diagrams are popular and useful graphic organizers for compare-and-contrast tasks. They are organizational devices with two or more overlapping circles for charting similarities (comparisons) and differences (contrasts) between characters in a story, ideas explained in an essay or lecture, two opposing points of view, and so on. Students may work individually, with partners, or in groups to examine a text or compose one using the Venn diagram format. The word *Venn* is capitalized because it is named after a famous mathematician who, among other interests, specialized in set theory; some of his work showing how the Venn diagram is used may be found online for free. Students label the diagram with the names of the two entities under analysis. They are shown how to list the elements particular to each entity in the outer parts of the circles. Within the overlap of the circles, they place the information common to both entities. This information may be recorded in note form or in sentences and may include illustrations. Venn diagram generators can be found online at www.readwritethink.org/files/resources/interactives/venn_diagrams and www.venngen.com. Learn how PowerPoint can be used to create Venn diagrams at http://office.microsoft.com/en-us/templates/venn-diagram-examples-TC101875471.aspx.

Venn diagrams definitely have their uses, but sometimes they may not encourage students to look deeply at a text or other information source. The overlapping portions of the circle are also difficult at times for students to write inside of. Consider the Venn diagram in Figure 6-13.

FIGURE 6-13
Venn Diagram for
S. E. Hinton's *The Outsiders*

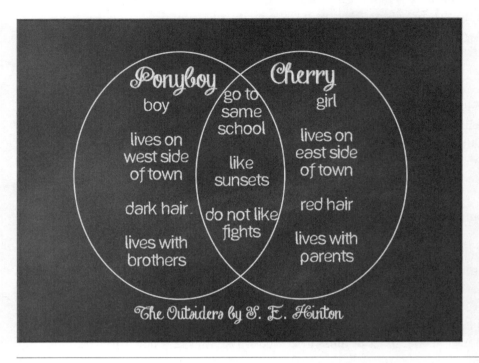

Source: Created by Stacy Miller.

The items compared are all accurate, but few of them really explore anything more than the surface-level identifying features of the characters Ponyboy and Cherry. Who they are as characters still lies buried and invisible to the reader and to those with whom the Venn diagram is shared. What can a teacher do about that? It is all about the attributes that are really important, the values they share, their experiences living in different parts of a Midwestern city, and possibly what makes them approach those values and experiences in different ways. The attributes of the comparison are critical if compare and contrast is to be a worthwhile exercise.

Using the principle that compare-and-contrast graphic organizers can help students hone in on the attributes that are particularly relevant to the learning targets at hand, we constructed the compare-and-contrast attribute chart in Figure 6-14. Others are available online, and you can find our downloadable version at **www.corwin.com/ miningcomplextext/2-5.** On this organizer, students are asked to compare and contrast two or more things (e.g., ideas, characters in a novel, things in the physical world) using a framework of relevant attributes. In some cases, students might brainstorm a list of important attributes based on their own experiences or on prior learning in class. Sometimes the framework will be determined by content-specific conventions. For example, characters in a novel might be compared one with another based on their personal strengths and challenges, their interactions with others, moral uprightness, or other personality traits that might be important considerations as determined by the teacher or a framework from previous learning in class. In science, it sometimes surprises students that the image of the atom they hold in their heads has evolved over time and that the most current thinking may not be reflected in their mental models.

Name: **Date:**

Subjects:

Topic or Concepts:

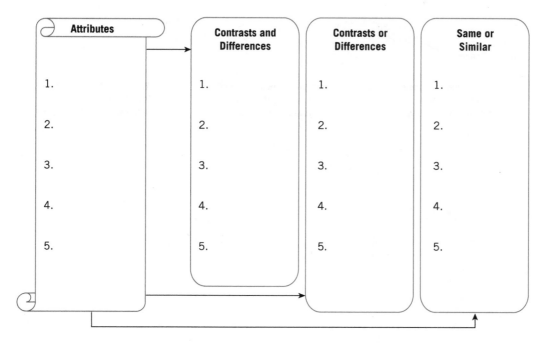

FIGURE 6-14
Compare-and-Contrast
Attribute Chart

Oh, one more thing. Earlier, we pointed out that there is a great deal of overlap between these text structures. We leave this topic with a connection question: How might compare-and-contrast attribute charts help students be more proficient with description?

Problem/Solution

What is the problem anyway? When working with problem/solution text structures, determining if there is a problem and the exact nature of the problem is the first step. In this way, the pattern aligns closely with inquiry modes of learning and the inquiry organizers found elsewhere in this book when students are the authors or makers of a product. When students read, they sometimes encounter a text that clearly identifies the problem and suggests one or more solutions. Often, however, the problem may be implied and the solutions not identified as such. Students must grapple with the text to identify the pattern. A graphic organizer for problem/solution may help guide the reader to determine if there is a problem discussed in the text, what that problem is, and what the solutions may be.

Example: English Language Arts

Gerald McDermott's (1972) classic, *Anansi the Spider: A Tale From the Ashanti*, is a perfect picture book to explore problem/solution text patterns. In the folk tale, Anansi runs into a bit of trouble, and his six sons rescue him using their particular gifts and talents. Later,

Anansi must decide which of his sons will receive the globe of light as a prize; the solution follows the traditional creation myth pattern, with Anansi acting the typical trickster archetype. Using the problem/solution organizer, Figure 6-15, students can track the problems the sons face in rescuing Anansi, and the final problem Anansi faces as he seeks to reward six sons with just one prize.

FIGURE 6-15
Problem/Solution
Graphic Organizer

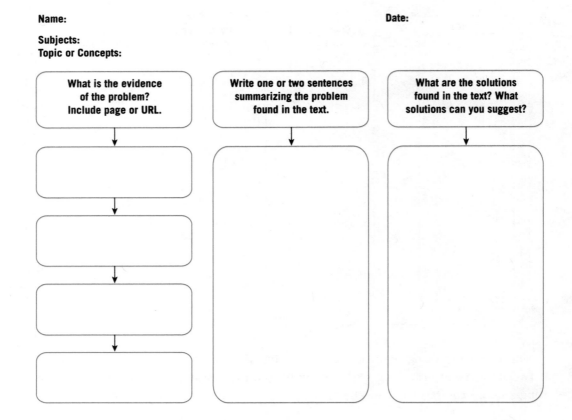

Name:

Date:

Subjects:
Topic or Concepts:

What is the evidence of the problem? Include page or URL.

Write one or two sentences summarizing the problem found in the text.

What are the solutions found in the text? What solutions can you suggest?

CCSS Anchor Standards (plus Standard 10)

CCSS.ELA-Literacy.CCRA.R.2.
Determine central ideas or themes of a text and analyze their development; summarize the key supporting details and ideas.

CCSS.ELA-Literacy.CCRA.R.5.
Analyze the structure of texts, including how specific sentences, paragraphs, and larger portions of the text (e.g., a section, chapter, scene, or stanza) relate to each other and the whole.

How Do I Use Top-Level Text Structures as Graphic Organizers?

- Determine the top-level text structure, or ask students to draw on their prior experience with text to determine what the top-level structure is for a given piece.
- Use the graphic organizer that is appropriate to the top-level structure as a means of guiding student reading.

- After students read and complete the graphic organizer, they may work in small groups to compare the information and perhaps adjust any aspects of the organizer based on their discussion.
- With teacher guidance or on their own, students should discuss or note how the organization of the text helps them learn what the text may be trying to convey.
- Use these organizers to help students respond to and construct text-dependent questions.

INTO THE CLASSROOM

Fourth Grade—Text Structure

CCSS.ELA-Literacy.RI.4.5.
Describe the overall structure (e.g., chronology, comparison, cause/effect, problem/solution) of events, ideas, concepts, or information in a text or part of a text.

CCSS.ELA-Literacy.RI.4.1.
Refer to details and examples in a text when explaining what the text says explicitly and when drawing inferences from the text.

CCSS.ELA-Literacy.W.4.1a.
Introduce a topic or text clearly, state an opinion, and create an organizational structure in which related ideas are grouped to support the writer's purpose.

THIS CLASSROOM EXAMPLE ADDRESSES THESE STANDARDS

Determining the Need

In fourth grade, students are challenged to read for top-level text types as a way of understanding and comprehending the material. Mrs. Dai's fourth graders had been building on what they learned in third grade about some text types, and they could readily recognize cause/effect, compare and contrast, and sequential patterns. The students used this information to help them set a purpose for their reading. Now, the students were ready to explore problem/solution structures. However, Mrs. Dai did not tell them what structure they were going to explore in their reading today.

Mrs. Dai asked her students if they could recall any informational books or articles they had read recently in class or at home that compared two or more things. Several students volunteered. She asked for examples of texts in sequence structures and in the cause/effect structure. Each time, the students came up with many responses from their reading. Then Mrs. Dai asked if there might be other top-level text structures, and the students agreed that there probably were others.

Introducing It

As part of their science curriculum, students read many texts about endangered species and habitat protection. An article in *Ranger Rick* magazine (www.nwf.org/Kids/Ranger-Rick.aspx) titled "Operation Woodpecker" provided just the reading material students needed to meet the science objective and the English language arts standards for fourth grade. Mrs. Dai asked students to read the comic-style article to learn more about the red-cockaded woodpecker and how it thrives on a military post in North Carolina. She also asked them to look for the text structure, though they did not yet know what that structure was. She also introduced some key words, such as *camp* as a reference to a type of military post.

Guided and Independent Practice

As students read "Operation Woodpecker," they learned many things about how this bird protects itself against predators, and what the Marines are doing to protect the woodpecker that lives in the trees at Camp Lejeune. After reading "Operation Woodpecker" once, students met in small groups to determine what the text structure might be. Even though the article was in a story form, they realized that the sequence of events was not the main idea of the piece. A few wondered if the structure was cause/effect because the woodpeckers are endangered and the Marines seemed to be helping to change that. In one group, Jayson thought for a moment, then said, "It seems there is a problem here. The woodpeckers are rare and the military wants to help them survive."

Kaela chimed right in. "You know, I think you're right. There is a problem. Aren't the Marines trying to solve the problem by creating the nest cavities in place?"

Jayson thought that sounded right and added, "The Marines are also marking trees where woodpeckers live so that they don't disturb the birds."

Later, Mrs. Dai asked students what they thought. Jayson and Kaela's group reported that this text structure must have something to do with solving problems. They were on the right track, and Mrs. Dai handed students a graphic organizer they could use to identify the problems and solutions they found when they reread the article. Jayson and Kaela's group produced the organizer seen in Figure 6-16.

FIGURE 6-16
Problem/Solution Graphic Organizer for a Science Article

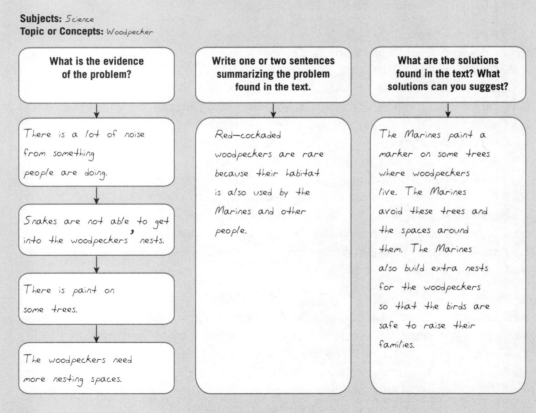

Subjects: *Science*
Topic or Concepts: *Woodpecker*

What is the evidence of the problem?	**Write one or two sentences summarizing the problem found in the text.**	**What are the solutions found in the text? What solutions can you suggest?**
There is a lot of noise from something people are doing.	Red-cockaded woodpeckers are rare because their habitat is also used by the Marines and other people.	The Marines paint a marker on some trees where woodpeckers live. The Marines avoid these trees and the spaces around them. The Marines also build extra nests for the woodpeckers so that the birds are safe to raise their families.
Snakes are not able to get into the woodpeckers' nests.		
There is paint on some trees.		
The woodpeckers need more nesting spaces.		

Closure

As students reread the article, they completed the graphic organizer in small groups. Mrs. Dai provided formative feedback as they worked on their organizers. The feedback focused on any misconceptions or missing information students displayed. To extend their understanding of a problem/solution structure, students next read and discussed several pieces incorporating this structure. They were then asked to identify a problem related to habitat protection and endangered species. Once the identification was made, they were tasked to write a solution to the problem using the class blog. In preparation they were encouraged to create a graphic that supported the development of the information they would share. It is so important to invite students to select or create organizers they will use to share their ideas. This promotes deeper thinking about the organization of the information they will be sharing.

Reading, Writing, and Discussion Extensions

The text structures discussed in this chapter are useful for students who are still learning to recognize the patterns and the information those patterns convey when students read. However, these structures are also useful for students as they think about their own written and multimodal compositions. Ask students to go beyond the top-level structure and consider how description fits into a composition that is basically a cause/effect exploration, for example. These structures are useful as students organize a composition in written or multimodal formats (see Sundeen, 2007). Lorenz, Green, and Brown (2009) found that average readers in primary grades benefited from the use of graphic organizers to give structure to their written work. Often, top-level text structures are a starting point for informing what students know and can do with a given text, but the organizers that represent those structures often pair well with other organizers. For example, problem/solution organizers may be an effective preliminary tool that can lead to inquiry organizers such as the I-chart and I-guide, which we discuss in the next chapter.

Photo by Thinkstock

GRAPHIC ORGANIZERS BOOST QUESTIONING AND RESPONDING

Inherent in the Common Core State Standards (Common Core State Standards Initiative, 2010b) is the notion that students are inquirers. Part of their identities as individuals resides in the possibility that they want to know more about the world they inhabit and the world they want to change in positive ways. Several Common Core standards ask that students look closely at the texts they read, the media they view, the compositions they create, and then ask questions about those texts. The graphic organizers in this chapter support their doing so.

I-CHART AND I-GUIDE

CCSS.ELA-Literacy.CCRA.R.7.

Integrate and evaluate content presented in diverse media and formats, including visually and quantitatively, as well as in words.

CCSS.ELA-Literacy.CCRA.R.8.

Delineate and evaluate the argument and specific claims in a text, including the validity of the reasoning as well as the relevance and sufficiency of the evidence.

CCSS.ELA-Literacy.CCRA.R.9.

Analyze how two or more texts address similar themes or topics in order to build knowledge or to compare the approaches the authors take.

What Are I-Charts and I-Guides?

Inquiry. It is one of those words that means many different things depending on the context, whom you ask, and when you ask just what *inquiry* means. We argue that inquiry can be, and often is, the soul of learning; when there are intriguing questions and a multiplicity of sources, students might be engaged and want to learn. In this section, we examine two organizers that usefully guide students to think about how inquiry extends learning tasks into the interesting, the useful, and the captivating. The first is the I-chart (I standing for inquiry; Hoffman, 1992) and the second is the I-guide (Wood, Lapp, Flood, & Taylor, 2008). As readers, you might recognize that there are parallels with the KWL format (Ogle, 1986) examined earlier in this book as well. If so, you are on the road to inquiry, the road that shows how ideas connect one with the other and sometimes where there are disconnects, too. Working with the many sources available in digital and more traditional environments is a hallmark of learning for millennial generation students. How those sources are evaluated as to their trustworthiness and how they fit, or don't fit, together is paramount for learners in today's schools as they work with multiple sources (Wood, 1998), make connections among sources, and compare concepts and texts.

To take an inquiry stance, in academic worlds, is to wonder. It is to notice that we know and can learn a great many things, but we typically end up with new questions, challenges to long-held assumptions, and creative or innovative solutions to vexing problems. The I-chart and I-guide build on this very notion. How else can we ask the tough questions of our lives except by inquiring, wondering, and questioning?

With the I-chart (Figure 7-1), students identify a topic, often in negotiation against learning goals, with the teacher and each other (Hoffman, 1992). They place their learning from various sources in relation to the questions and subquestions they generate as they investigate texts. The I-guide (Figure 7-2) builds on this approach by asking students to develop a reading plan, identify the major themes from their reading, and then synthesize the texts with which they interact (Wood et al., 2008).

How Do I Use an I-Chart or I-Guide?

- Choose the I-guide or I-chart format. The I-guide favors overarching themes and questions, while the I-chart concentrates student attention on specific subquestions.

FIGURE 7-1
I-Chart

What We Know						
	Topic	Question	Question	Question	Other Interesting Facts and Figures	New Questions
Sources						
Synthesis						

FIGURE 7-2
I-Guide

What We Know					
	Topic or Question	Major Subtopics or Themes		Summary of Each Text	Importance or Relevance of the Information
Sources					
Synthesis					

- Determine what resources students are allowed to use, and ensure they have the research skills and reading capacities to make sense of the materials they encounter.
- Model the use of the chart or guide using a familiar topic.
- Allow students to use the chart or guide to work on and shape their research.
- Determine the final product that demonstrates the processes they used in the inquiry and their newfound understanding.

The I-chart and I-guide formats provide a visual format students might use to guide their inquiry and provide a sense of purpose for their readings.

INTO THE CLASSROOM

Fourth Grade—Extreme Weather

THIS CLASSROOM EXAMPLE ADDRESSES THESE STANDARDS

CCSS.ELA-Literacy.RI.4.9.
Integrate information from two texts on the same topic in order to write or speak about the subject knowledgeably.

CCSS.ELA-Literacy.W.4.2.
Write informative/explanatory texts to examine a topic and convey ideas and information clearly.

Determining the Need

Mrs. Mordecai's fourth graders explored the effects of waves, wind, water, and ice on Earth's features. They were very interested in Hurricane Sandy, which had recently caused so much destruction in their part of the world. When they read an article in *SuperScience* about efforts to protect against some of the effects of future hurricanes, they wanted to know more. The I-guide gave them the opportunity to use that source and explore others as they looked for the major themes related to their question: How might communities protect themselves against future destruction by such harsh weather?

Because Mrs. Mordecai's students wanted to know more about how their communities could protect themselves from future storms, they brainstormed some background knowledge they already knew from the news and from watching what was going on around town. They noticed that new dunes of sand were being built by heavy equipment, for example.

Introducing It

The students had observed many things around town, and they had read the *SuperScience* article. Mrs. Mordecai knew that they needed to read even more to obtain more information and compare the sources. She introduced the I-guide and showed them how to use it. Together, Mrs. Mordecai and her students filled in the first row using the *SuperScience* article as a foundation. Then she directed students to two other articles they might find helpful. She also told students that they could look for additional sources using ipl2's For Kids search tool to search with the key word *hurricane* (www.ipl.org/div/kidspace).

Guided and Independent Practice

Students began reading the articles. Each student created his or her own I-guide, then in groups students compiled their individual I-guides into one I-guide for their group. Discussion, the students knew, helped them refine their ideas. Figure 7-3 shows the I-guide from one group. The next step was to prepare a presentation using PowerPoint or another presentation tool which they would place on the class web page for others, including their parents, to view and to comment on.

FIGURE 7-3
Example of Student's
I-Guide on Erosion

What We Know					
• There is lots of work being done around town to build dunes. • Christmas trees are being dumped around the beach. • Lots of people died and houses were ruined.					
	Topic or Question	Major Subtopics or Themes		Summary of Each Text	Importance or Relevance of the Information
Sources	Super Science	Lots of erosion	People build sand dunes	Climate change gives us more problems	Erosion led people to build dunes, but the problem is going to continue	Helpful
	Superstorm Sandy Facts	Many people died (at least 149)	No power for many others	High winds	The weather caused many problems, including damage to property and deaths	Kind of helpful
	Sandy's Aftermath	Sandy collided with an Arctic storm. Other weather stopped Sandy from going to sea.	Some people trapped in their homes	High winds and water	The storm was worse because of other weather conditions, and there were many people hurt because of the storm	Kind of helpful, hard to read
Synthesis	All articles agreed that many people died and many others lost their property. Only one focused on efforts to prevent this kind of damage in the future.				

After students shared their I-guides and their final presentations, Mrs. Mordecai asked them to post an entry on the class blog about how they worked with others to compare information from several sources and eventually synthesize the information from several places.

Reading, Writing, and Discussion Extensions

Inquiry is often thought of as a process that generally results in some kind of product (e.g., report, presentation, model). In what ways might I-charts and I-guides contribute to comprehension processes as students read to learn and provide evidence of that learning in written work or in discussion? How might I-charts and I-guides relate to text structures, especially problem/solution? What does inquiry have to do with opinion and argumentation and the organizers you will find later in this book? These questions are meant to encourage you to invite and support students in moving toward independence is selecting and creating graphic organizers that will best represent their thinking, interpretations, and presentations of information.

FLIP CHART MANIPULATIVE

THIS ORGANIZER ADDRESSES THESE STANDARDS

What Is a Flip Chart Manipulative?

A flip chart, a type of manipulative strategy guide (see Wood et al., 2008), can be a powerful way for students to organize information about a unit of study. Flip charts are easy to make, and each page can display information on a variety of topics. Flip charts can be used to create story maps, organize information for a research project, and display information about different books that allow for comparisons across texts and so much more!

Example: Mathematics

Flip charts can easily be adapted to mathematical topics. Teachers can use a flip chart to make a student-friendly version of the eight mathematical practices (see Figure 7-4).
"Do I understand what the problem is asking?" is written on the first tab. On that page, students can draw or write different ways of reading problems and how they know they have the correct information to solve the problem. On the second tab, students can draw examples of different ways to solve a problem. The third tab says "How can I prove my problem is correct?" On the inside of this tab, students can draw other ways of solving problems, such as objects, drawings, diagrams, and actions, as well as write clarifying questions they can ask each other.

How Do I Use a Flip Chart Manipulative?

- Stack three to five sheets of paper on top of one another with a half-inch overlap.
- Fold in the middle.
- Staple the top just below the fold.

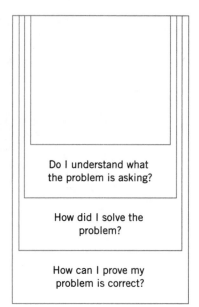

FIGURE 7-4
Math Flip Chart

Do I understand what the problem is asking?

How did I solve the problem?

How can I prove my problem is correct?

CCSS.ELA-Literacy.CCRA.R.2.

Determine central ideas or themes of a text and analyze their development; summarize the key supporting details and ideas.

During her narrative unit, Mrs. Brown wanted to know if her second-grade students understood the characters, setting, plot, and author's purpose for the books they read. She created an activity that all her students could do, no matter what their reading level.

Introducing It

Before the unit began, Mrs. Brown showed each of her students how to make a flip chart and label the tabs. The labels for this particular unit were *characters, setting, plot,* and *author's purpose.* As Mrs. Brown taught each skill during her mini-lesson, she modeled for her students how to fill out each tab.

Guided and Independent Practice

When students independently read during reader's workshop, they read their own "just right" books and filled out the appropriate tab.

Closure

At the end of the unit, Mrs. Brown collected each flip chart and assessed students' understanding of each element. Students met in conference with Mrs. Brown to review any areas that seemed to present a problem or to challenge them to continue their explorations of these concepts.

Reading, Writing, and Discussion Extensions

Not only do students read the text they are considering in science, social studies, literature, and other subjects as they construct their flip charts, but they also may use them to discuss the literature they have read. The flip charts become a visual aid as students compare thoughts and ideas in small-group discussions. Other organizers in this book help students see how discipline-specific patterns can help them understand how scientists organize their work, how historians make sense of many documents, or how readers understand and talk about the fiction they read. We like the manipulative aspects of the flip chart because students like to fold paper and because it helps them through tactile means to understand how knowledge is organized.

TEXT-DEPENDENT
QUESTION/RESPONSE ORGANIZER

CCSS.ELA-Literacy.CCRA.R.1.

Read closely to determine what the text says explicitly and to make logical inferences from it; cite specific textual evidence when writing or speaking to support conclusions drawn from the text.

CCSS.ELA-Literacy.CCRA.R.10.

Read and comprehend complex literary and informational texts independently and proficiently.

THIS ORGANIZER ADDRESSES THESE STANDARDS

What Is a Text-Dependent Question/Response Organizer?

Name: **Date:**
Subject:

| Circle one:
 • This is my first reading
 • Second reading
 • Third or more readings | The text-dependent question is: |

After reading the text again, I found this evidence to support my answer (with page numbers):

And now my response to the question is:

FIGURE 7-5
Text-Dependent
Question/Response
Organizer

To achieve Common Core State Standards and other rigorous goals for learning, students must attend more fully to the words on the page or screen. As students read, they need thinking structures that assist them to work through complex texts. Close reading and text-dependent questions work together to help students understand just what the words on the page tell the reader. Though what students know and bring to the page is critically essential, what they can make of the words, sentences, and larger blocks of text they encounter is of particular importance as well. Text-dependent questions are one way to guide students to just what those words might convey. Though these questions can be quite literal or involve analysis, the graphic organizers presented here focus on inference, and not just any type of inference. Our colleagues Doug Fisher and Nancy Frey (2012b) present a continuum of text-dependent questions that include attention to general understandings, key details, vocabulary, text structure, and author's purpose at the lower end of the continuum. While the top level of their graphic helps students make inferences, intertextual connections, and attend to the construction of opinions and arguments, this is not intended to be a hierarchical model. The question to be asked depends on the lesson purpose and the students' knowledge. Notice that, whereas other organizers in this book focus on five of the six levels of this continuum, this graphic organizer (Figure 7-4) zeroes in on text-dependent questions that help build student capacity to make and work with inferences.

Questions seem so natural to teachers and students that it sometimes seems there is no need to plan them, but that may not be the case. If students are to learn to make useful inferences as they read, teachers much avoid asking too many literal-level questions at the expense of those that require higher-level thinking, such as those required in making an inference (see Daines, 1986; Fisher & Frey, 2012b). With careful planning, teachers can ask text-dependent questions that scaffold student thinking with complex texts. We think it is important to note that questions are not always deployed just to assess what students know and can do; very often, questions can guide students to the intended cognitive skill as they make inferences along the way.

As readers who are familiar with the question–answer relationship strategy know, Raphael (1984, 1986) highlights four types of questions students might generate or to which they might be asked to respond: right there, think and search, author and me, and on my own. The purpose of identifying the question type is that this information guides students to know what they are to do in order to gain deeper and deeper insights about the information in the text. In the first two question types, students rely on information directly in the text at the literal and textually implicit level. In the third and fourth question types, students relate what they know from background or prior knowledge and match that to what they are actually reading in the text. Questions that call for students to make textually implicit assumptions or inferences in order to determine an appropriate response from two or more parts of the text are textually implicit and termed "think and search," or sometimes "figure it out." Questions that ask students to draw on their background or prior knowledge and join that with what they have read are known as "author and me" questions. The real kicker is that to understand the question and respond to it, students must have read the text and be able to use evidence from it in order to respond. Using evidence from the text is the foundation of close reading strategies and the text-dependent questions that promote the capacity to make increasing sophisticated inferences across grade-levels and with complex texts in various disciplines.

Authors imply, and readers infer. Thus, what authors say, hint at, or believe their audiences already know is very important when students are asked to actively look for and construct inferences based on what the text actually states. Even though inferences are constructed at almost every level (e.g., word level, sentence level) as a reader approaches a text, the text-dependent question response organizer focuses on larger blocks of text at the paragraph, chapter, and whole-text levels. In many close reading schemes (see Fisher, Frey, & Lapp, 2012), students read a text multiple times with a different, scaffolded focus on each reading. Often, the use of text-dependent questions appears after students have read a text two or more times. Thus, they are familiar with the content, and they are now working actively to make inferences.

Text-dependent question/response organizers may make the process of inferring visible to students who have a tough time with this task (notice we did not use the made-up word *inferencing* when *inferring* will do just fine!). In the close reading process, students have already read the text under consideration, and now they are looking at the nuances of the inferences they have already made and the details from the text and from their own background knowledge that they brought to the reading.

How Do I Use a Text-Dependent Question/Response Organizer?

- Text-dependent questions focus students' attention on particular aspects of a text, and in this case, inferences are at the foreground. In close reading, students have already read the text at hand at least one time, sometimes more. The inferential question they are asked helps them think about what the text actually conveys and how they may gather information to further deepen their knowledge through close reading of that text.
- Ask a text-dependent question that requires inferences to be made at different points in the text.
- Students, who have already read the material at least once, then note an initial inference that responds to the question.
- Next, they go back to the text to find specific evidence from multiple points in it that help them build a chain of indicators that support the inference or cause them to adjust the inference they originally made.
- Students discuss their responses to the text-dependent question in groups and then compare their responses with other groups.

INTO THE CLASSROOM

Fifth Grade—Inferring While Reading

CCSS.ELA-Literacy.RL.5.1.
Quote accurately from a text when explaining what the text says explicitly and when drawing inferences from the text.

THIS CLASSROOM EXAMPLE ADDRESSES THESE STANDARDS

CCSS.ELA-Literacy.RL.5.10.
By the end of the year, read and comprehend literature, including stories, dramas, and poetry, at the high end of the grades 4–5 text complexity band independently and proficiently.

Struggling with a text, Ms. Pereiria, came to know, is not always detrimental. Tough texts sometimes mean that students are challenged but are capable of meeting that challenge. Some of her students just needed the appropriate scaffolding to be successful with inferences, particularly the textually implicit type that relied on how students connected ideas in any given piece as they read. She knew her students were capable of struggling through a text and that such a struggle often resulted in high-quality learning.

Determining the Need

Based on previous assessment data, Ms. Pereiria identified some students who were still having a difficult time making inferences when reading complex texts with Lexiles appropriate for their grade level: fifth grade. She gathered them at a table in her room while other students pursued other academic tasks. The students were used to meeting with Ms. Pereiria for all kinds of tasks, including acceleration, interest-based projects, and so on. Each student had a tablet computer with a digital copy of *Ghost Ship on the Cay: A 15-Minute Ghost Story* (Alexander, 2007). Ms. Pereiria previewed several vocabulary words (e.g., *hull, ship's log, keel*) and told students that there were some other words they would need to figure out (e.g., *provisions, providence*). The students began reading, then they partnered up with a buddy and summarized the story.

Introducing It

Modeling is an important part of teaching students how to read a text closely. During a previous whole-class close reading experience, Ms. Pereiria determined that this group of students would benefit from additional modeling before they could engage in close reading that didn't involve her frontloading of vocabulary and other supports. Because of this assessment she was now working with them in a smaller group to interactively model and practice the process of close reading. Once students finished their discussions, she modeled the inferences she made by discussing the first two pages. She told students that she was initially sure the ship was going to crash into the rocks, and maybe a lot of people would die and become ghosts. But when she read the last paragraph on the page, she made a new inference:

> Seeing the size of the wave, the villagers turned and ran. When they stopped to look back, they saw a sight which filled them with awe. There sat the ship, high upon the sandy beach. Its keel sunk deep into the sandy shore. (p. 4)

Her new inference was that the ghosts were already on the ship. She and the students turned the virtual page. Together they analyzed the language that indicated that her inference was correct. They told her they, too, had already realized this from their first reading. Ms. Pereiria posed two additional questions that caused students to return to the text to find information by making inferences. Next, they discussed their thinking and what prompted it as Ms. Pereiria wrote the inferences and evidence they noted on chart paper for students to see.

Guided and Independent Practice

Finally, Ms. Pereiria handed students the text-dependent question/response organizer and asked them, "Even though the captain had written in his log that the ship might be doomed, what do you think happened to the crew? No bodies, except for Jack's, were on board. Be sure to support your responses with insights from the text." The students wrote the question on their organizers, reread the text, and wrote brief responses to the question. A few students made guesses that were not supported by the story, such as "Aliens beamed them off the ship." That was fine, Ms. Pereiria thought; they will adjust their thinking as they reread the text. When they were finished, they went back to their tablet computers and read the story one more time on their own and noted evidence from the story.

Closure

Most of the students were then able to fine-tune their inferences based on the evidence from the story. The most popular inference supported by the evidence in the text was that the crew was swept overboard by a big wave, much like the one that brought the ship to Brighton Cay, where Jack's mother lived, a year later. As Ms. Pereiria listened to students' thinking, she felt secure that they had learned how to use the text to support making inferences. She always encouraged students to add information after the collaborative conversations because it is through these rich conversations about the text information that their initial thinking is enhanced.

Reading, Writing, and Discussion Extensions

Many of the students in Ms. Pereiria's class had heard and even told ghost stories. This provided a perfect opportunity for writing. Now that they had read this ghost story, Ms. Pereiria challenged students to find another ghost story in the school library, the digital collections on their tablets, or online. She had in mind standard CCSS.ELA-Literacy.W.5.2, "Write informative/explanatory texts to examine a topic and convey ideas and information clearly," when she asked them to write a short paper comparing the two ghost stories they had read and to find commonalities among the stories. Encouraged that all of the students, including the small group with whom she had worked, had learned the structure of story, she believed they could blend this information with what they had previously learned about the compare-and-contrast text structure to craft this comparative example. She invited students to use a graphic organizer to help organize their thinking about the information.

Photo by Thinkstock

GRAPHIC ORGANIZERS FOSTER READING, FORMING, AND WRITING OPINIONS

A new focus for young writers in elementary grades is that they form opinions based on the sources they read and can consult in other ways. This chapter examines how the Common Core State Standards (2010b) call for students to move from their own observations to consultation of sources as they form opinions that they express in writing and other multimodal compositions.

ANCHOR STANDARD 1 ACROSS THE GRADES

CCSS.ELA-Literacy.CCRA.W.1

Write arguments to support claims in an analysis of substantive topics or texts using valid reasoning and relevant and sufficient evidence.

The Primary Years

Grade K

CCSS.ELA-Literacy.W.K.1.

Use a combination of drawing, dictating, and writing **to compose opinion pieces** in which they tell a reader the topic or the name of the book they are writing about and state an opinion or preference about the topic or book (e.g., *My favorite book is . . .*).

Grade 1

CCSS.ELA-Literacy.W.1.1.

Write opinion pieces in which they introduce the topic or name the book they are writing about, state an opinion, supply a reason for the opinion, and provide some sense of closure.

Grade 2

CCSS.ELA-Literacy.W.2.1.

Write opinion pieces in which they introduce the topic or book they are writing about, state an opinion, supply reasons that support the opinion, use linking words (e.g., *because, and, also*) to connect opinion and reasons, and provide a concluding statement or section.

As you read through this progression of the Common Core State Standards, please note the increase in performance expectations that is called out in bolded font. Students are first asked to state and write opinions. They move from providing opinions in kindergarten to providing introductions, including readings for opinions, and then writing a concluding statement in first grade. Word choice is increasingly important across the grade levels.

The Intermediate Years

Grade 3

CCSS.ELA-Literacy.W.3.1.

Write opinion pieces on topics or texts, supporting a point of view with reasons.

CCSS.ELA-Literacy.W.3.1a.

Introduce the topic or text they are writing about, state an opinion, and **create an organizational structure that lists reasons.**

CCSS.ELA-Literacy.W.3.1b.

Provide reasons that support the opinion.

CCSS.ELA-Literacy.W.3.1c.

Use linking words and phrases (e.g., *because, therefore, since, for example*) to connect opinion and reasons.

Provide a concluding statement or section.

These standards build on the work students do in kindergarten through second grade, but they accelerate things in such a way that students must now assume a point of view. The organizational structures they use in composition moves from words to phrases as they link important ideas.

Grade 4

Write opinion pieces on topics or texts, supporting a point of view with reasons **and information.**

Introduce a topic or text clearly, state an opinion, and **create an organizational structure in which related ideas are grouped to support the writer's purpose.**

Provide reasons that are **supported by facts and details.**

Link opinion and reasons using words and phrases (e.g., *for instance, in order to, in addition*).

Provide a concluding statement or section **related to the opinion presented.**

Grade 5

Write opinion pieces on topics or texts, supporting a point of view with reasons and information.

Introduce a topic or text clearly, **state an opinion,** and create an organizational structure in which ideas are logically grouped to support the writer's purpose.

Provide **logically ordered reasons** that are supported by facts and details.

Link opinion and reasons using words, phrases, and clauses (e.g., *consequently, specifically*).

Provide a concluding statement or section related to the opinion presented.

In Grades 4 and 5, students create more sophisticated writing products. They must support points of view with reasons, information, facts, and details and include a conclusion. Organizational structures should include ideas that are strategically grouped and logically ordered. Opinions and reasons must be linked using increasingly sophisticated language units inclusive of words, phrases, and clauses.

The Middle School Years

This book focuses on second through fifth grades, but where students are going is as vitally important as where they have been. More formal structures found in argumentation become important at this level.

CCSS.ELA-Literacy.W.K.6.1.

Write arguments to support claims with clear reasons and relevant evidence.

CCSS.ELA-Literacy.W.6.1a.

Introduce claim(s) and organize the reasons and evidence clearly.

CCSS.ELA-Literacy.W.6.1b.

Support claim(s) with clear reasons and relevant evidence, using credible sources and demonstrating an understanding of the topic or text.

CCSS.ELA-Literacy.W.6.1c.

Use words, phrases, and clauses to clarify the relationships among claim(s) and reasons.

CCSS.ELA-Literacy.W.6.1d.

Establish and maintain a formal style.

CCSS.ELA-Literacy.W.6.1e.

Provide a concluding statement or section that follows from the argument presented.

In sixth grade the writing of opinions moves toward the construction of arguments in which students support claims with text-based evidence. They employ formal organizational structures of argument, including claims, reasons, evidence, and credible sources, along with words, phrases, and clauses that link relationships among claims and reasons. In middle school, students become aware of the need to establish and write in a formal style. Graphic organizers support this learning.

SIX-PART OPINION ORGANIZER

What Is a Six-Part Opinion Organizer?

FIGURE 8-1
Six-Part Opinion
Organizer

Explain an opinion you have about this topic:	
Topic:	
Opinion:	
1. My current position is:	**2. What I think the position of others might be:**
3. The response of others to my opinion could be:	**4. My response to them is:**
5. How do I know?	**6. How has my opinion changed?**

Every human being we have ever encountered in our journeys through life has an opinion. Opinions, we find, are ever changing and simultaneously somewhat fixed. The happy challenge teachers face is that they can help their students form opinions that carry some weight because they are well grounded in background knowledge, experience and observation, and knowledge gained from other sources in forming that opinion. In other words, opinions are not always based on evidence, but the most useful opinions typically are. That is where graphic organizers come in. Gallagher (2011) proposes the four-square argument, a means of assisting students to look at the opposing sides of an argument—not just to counter the opposing side, but to inform their own opinions and arguments as well. In the graphic organizer in Figure 8-1, we adapt Gallagher's four-square argument chart a bit for general use in elementary grades and to guide students to look beyond their own situations to the world outside. This six-part opinion chart includes a section for students to note the sources they consult as their opinions develop.

How Do I Use the Six-Part Opinion Organizer?

- Students need to know, and the teacher should reinforce, the idea that opinions are everywhere. Some opinions are not based on evidence and may not consider alternative information or points of view.
- Ask students to generate opinions about a topic that is relevant to the curriculum and content under study.
- Remind students that they may need to change their opinions once they have considered the topic from other points of view. The six-part opinion organizer might be used with the multiple source organizers elsewhere in this book, such as the I-guide (see Chapter 7) and the thinking map (see the next section of this chapter).
- As students consult various sources, they should include their notes on the organizer, noting how their opinions coincide with and differ from those of others and how their own opinions change.
- Next, students can create a product in writing or multimodal formats to be shared showing how their thinking changed or was reinforced as they consulted other sources.

INTO THE CLASSROOM

Fifth Grade—Opinion Writing

Determining the Need

Mr. Lassuire was tired of the same old opinion essays that asked students to argue that homework should be curtailed or that recess should be longer. Using the six-part opinion organizer format, he asked his students to look into real problems in the community. These included the lack of a bike lane on major roads, the hours of the community center that did not extend into the evening when kids really needed it, and the desire for a community garden at the school where space was available but not the resources to make it happen.

After brainstorming some issues students really cared about and writing them on the board, Mr. Lassuire had his students use the six-part opinion grid to identify their own opinions about a topic.

Introducing It

Mr. Lassuire knew that general Internet inquiries could be a challenge for students because they had so many variables to sift through in order to find information that they could read (Wolsey, Lapp, & Fisher, 2012) and that was relevant to the task. What he chose to do was a preliminary web search on the topics that interested the students, and then he posted those search results to the class web page, sorted by topic. Students could use those resources if they wished, and then they were allowed to conduct searches for more information using a kid-friendly search engine such as those listed at www.kidfriendlysearch.com/Kid_Friendly.htm.

Next, Mr. Lassuire asked students to fill in square one, "My current position is." Then he asked them to predict and fill out square two, "What I think the position of others might be." He reminded students that they should record their sources of information in square five, "How do I know" as they go. They could use the back of the graphic organizer if they wished to do so.

Guided and Independent Practice

After students had done some research on the Internet, in the school library, and sometimes by interviewing others in the community, they worked on the third and fourth squares: "The response of others to my opinion could be" and "My response to them is."

Students were intrigued to learn that often their ideas were very good but sometimes there were practical reasons why others might not be willing, at first, to make things happen. They composed their responses to the counter-opinions, then they proposed solutions or reactions based on what they learned on the six-part opinion grid. Throughout the process, they tracked their sources of information and noted how their own opinions had changed as they engaged in the public sphere with those whose opinions differed from their own.

Closure

Once students had formed their opinions, read to find support for those opinions, and also read to determine the opinions of others, they were ready to construct a presentation to the city council, compose a podcast, write a letter to the editor, or argue before the school board.

Reading, Writing, and Discussion Extensions

Throughout the process of forming an opinion, consulting other sources to confirm or disconfirm evidence or counter-opinions, students engaged with texts and people who could help them think about the opinions they held and how those opinions changed over time. In the example from Mr. Lassuire's classroom, students wrote letters to the newspaper and composed podcasts that they shared on the class web page. Using the six-part opinion organizer required students to consider multiple sources of information. Which other organizers in this book, or others you know of, help students work with multiple sources?

THINKING MAP

CCSS.ELA-Literacy.CCRA.R.6.

Assess how point of view or purpose shapes the content and style of a text.

CCSS.ELA-Literacy.CCRA.R.8.

Delineate and evaluate the argument and specific claims in a text, including the validity of the reasoning as well as the relevance and sufficiency of the evidence.

CCSS.ELA-Literacy.CCRA.W.1.

Write arguments to support claims in an analysis of substantive topics or texts using valid reasoning and relevant and sufficient evidence.

CCSS.ELA-Literacy.CCRA.W.8.

Gather relevant information from multiple print and digital sources, assess the credibility and accuracy of each source, and integrate the information while avoiding plagiarism.

CCSS.ELA-Literacy.CCRA.W.9.

Draw evidence from literary or informational texts to support analysis, reflection, and research.

THIS ORGANIZER ADDRESSES THESE STANDARDS

What Is a Thinking Map?

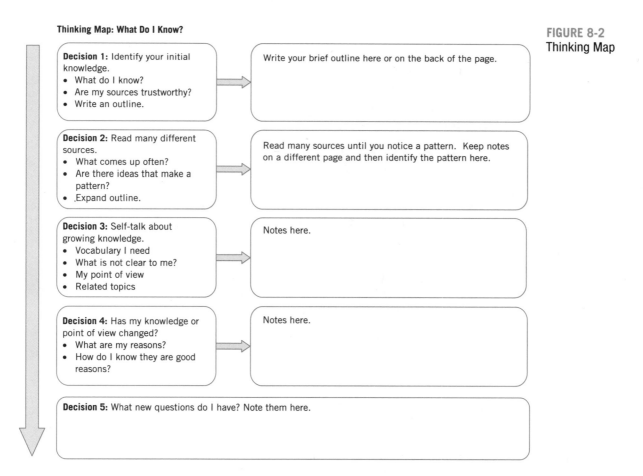

Thinking Map: What Do I Know?

Decision 1: Identify your initial knowledge.
- What do I know?
- Are my sources trustworthy?
- Write an outline.

Write your brief outline here or on the back of the page.

Decision 2: Read many different sources.
- What comes up often?
- Are there ideas that make a pattern?
- Expand outline.

Read many sources until you notice a pattern. Keep notes on a different page and then identify the pattern here.

Decision 3: Self-talk about growing knowledge.
- Vocabulary I need
- What is not clear to me?
- My point of view
- Related topics

Notes here.

Decision 4: Has my knowledge or point of view changed?
- What are my reasons?
- How do I know they are good reasons?

Notes here.

Decision 5: What new questions do I have? Note them here.

FIGURE 8-2
Thinking Map

A thinking map is a way for students to assess their own background knowledge relative to a given inquiry or classroom task. As students work with sources to compose their thinking and the multimodal or written products that accompany that thinking, they often find that they don't have the needed background knowledge. The thinking map is a means of guiding students through that process when they recognize they may need to develop their background knowledge through further reading and exploration of other sources.

How Do I Use a Thinking Map?

Model the process for students using the following decision points. The graphic organizer associated with the thinking map process will help students, step by step, to notice what they still need to learn and how to find that information.

Decision 1: Identify the topic.

- Ask yourself what you know about this topic.

   Make an outline of what you know. If you feel you don't have enough knowledge to assess the credibility of a site, stop and fill your knowledge bank. Ask yourself if the information in the source is true. If you cannot readily confirm the facts in the source, ask yourself if you would be able to find this information elsewhere. If the answer is yes, then you need to do more research.

Decision 2: Investigate and read many sources from various places.

- Determine the credibility and reliability of the source.
- Determine the sources with disconfirming or opposing points of view.
- Expand your outline. Summarize key points of each source. Identify positions which may conflict.

Decision 3: Talk to yourself throughout, evaluating your growing knowledge.

- What vocabulary do you need to develop?
- What concepts are not clear to you?
- What is your point of view? How does this differ from the point of view of others (especially for persuasive/opinion pieces)?
- What other fields or domains are related to your topic?

Decision 4: How has your knowledge or point of view changed?

How do you represent your new knowledge, your point of view, and the points of view of others in your writing and presentations?

Decision 5: What new questions do you have?

Fourth Grade—Learning to Ask and Research Relevant Questions

CCSS.ELA-Literacy.RI.4.6.

Compare and contrast a firsthand and secondhand account of the same event or topic; describe the differences in focus and the information provided.

CCSS.ELA-Literacy.RI.4.8.

Explain how an author uses reasons and evidence to support particular points in a text.

CCSS.ELA-Literacy.W.4.1.

Write opinion pieces on topics or texts, supporting a point of view with reasons and information.

CCSS.ELA-Literacy.W.4.8.

Recall relevant information from experiences or gather relevant information from print and digital sources; take notes and categorize information, and provide a list of sources.

CCSS.ELA-Literacy.W.4.9.

Draw evidence from literary or informational texts to support analysis, reflection, and research.

THIS CLASSROOM EXAMPLE ADDRESSES THESE STANDARDS

Determining the Need

Some of the brightest students Mrs. Okoro had ever had sat in her fourth-grade class, and they really wanted to know more about almost every topic they encountered. Sometimes they struggled with the ideas they encountered because they knew they needed to learn more than what they found in the required readings in science, social studies, and so on. Mrs. Okoro used the thinking map to help students recognize that they knew quite a lot about many things, but any knowledge they had led to new questions and additional readings and consultation with other sources.

Bones—everyone has them, and a few of Mrs. Okoro's students had even broken some of theirs. They knew a lot about those bones, but they were surprised to learn that sometimes bones can have a disease. Plus, there are things they could do to take care of the health of their bones.

Introducing It

Mrs. Okoro gave each student a graphic organizer. She and the students discussed whether the selected organizer matched their purpose. Then she modeled how to use it. Together, the students filled in the first box with what they already knew about bones and the skeleton. Then Mrs. Okoro showed students how to use Kids.gov (http://kids.usa.gov) to find information about the skeletal system.

Guided and Independent Practice

As students read through the results of their searches on Kids.gov, they made notes, recorded the sources of information, and looked for patterns that showed what was important and more likely to be reliable. They looked specifically for sources that discussed bone health and diseases as well as general facts. Students often worked together, but they created their own organizers and notes.

Next, students worked in small groups to compare the sources they found and the patterns that emerged. They wondered what was most important to do to take care of bone health and to avoid diseases. Finally, each student used the graphic organizer to show how his or her knowledge had changed and grown. Of course, students had new questions, and they added that to the Decision 5 section on the organizer as well.

Closure

Mrs. Okoro assessed each organizer formatively to identify any particular areas that might need to be corrected or enhanced through further instruction. For some students, she provided additional feedback to guide them in correcting misconceptions they encountered or to encourage further study.

Reading, Writing, and Discussion Extensions

Not only can students use the thinking map organizer to track their learning and note what they need to learn, they can also use it to prepare presentations for their peers and for online audiences. Doing so involves an interactive process of considering the information to be shared and contrasting it with the best organization to share it. Encouraging students to engage in this analytic thinking promotes their ability to truly understand and illustrate their ideas. Building background knowledge is not just something the teacher does for students. In the age of the Common Core State Standards, students are tasked to recognize what they know and what they still need to know in order to be well informed about the topics and questions they encounter. Connections to the modified KWL and I-charts and I-guides are helpful as students learn to take responsibility for their own learning.

GRAPHIC ORGANIZERS SUPPORT COLLABORATION

The point of literacy is and has to be how human beings interact one with another. In school, students are often asked to engage in collaborative projects. The quality of their interactions is vitally important if all students are to make use of the opportunities that collaboration provides. This chapter introduces a graphic organizer for managing larger projects.

PROJECT MANAGEMENT ORGANIZER

THIS ORGANIZER ADDRESSES THESE STANDARDS

CCSS.ELA-Literacy.CCRA.SL.1.

Prepare for and participate effectively in a range of conversations and collaborations with diverse partners, building on others' ideas and expressing their own clearly and persuasively.

CCSS.ELA-Literacy.CCRA.SL.6.

Adapt speech to a variety of contexts and communicative tasks, demonstrating command of formal English when indicated or appropriate.

What Is a Project Management Organizer?

In many classrooms, students work together on projects that take several days or even weeks to accomplish.[1] These projects include preparing presentations to the class, making a digital demonstration of knowledge, or engaging in various service learning activities. The Common Core State Standards in English language arts/literacy emphasize the capacity for students to work together in a variety of settings and contexts where literacy skills are necessary. As important is that such skills prepare students for college and career experiences where project management and planning skills are necessary for success.

A project management tool that has been around for more than a century is named after the man who created it, Henry Gantt (see Clark, 1923). The Gantt chart has been used in the military, in manufacturing industries, and in long-range planning just about everywhere, including schools. Gantt charts are useful because, graphically, "work planned and work done are shown in the same space in relation to each other and in their relation to time" (p. v). Their visual nature encourages student project participants to develop a plan, stick to it, and note their progress over time. Digital tools improve Gantt charts by automating some tasks, making them easily available to project participants at any time, and being infinitely expandable. The use of color further improves the look and feel of the organizer.

Gantt project management organizers can be created with sticky notes on a whiteboard, on butcher paper, or with an 11 × 17 piece of construction paper. In this chapter, we use Excel spreadsheets (see Figure 9-1), though the Gantt chart can easily be created in a shared spreadsheet file such as those found in Google Docs or with software specifically designed for this purpose (see Figure 9-2).

Smartsheet provides organizers for students and teachers at https://chrome.google.com/webstore/detail/smartsheet-group-project/kejkalfabljbhkapdinmjdhccbmofjio?hl=en and https://chrome.google.com/webstore/detail/smartsheet-class-syllabus/bnoamkimecefacafihefokmbhcjhnlpc?hl=en. These are best accessed using the Google Chrome web browser.

Templates for Gantt project management organizers are helpful because the setup is already done. A basic template from Microsoft downloads can be found at http://office.microsoft.com/en-us/templates/gantt-project-planner-TC102887601.aspx. In Figure 9-3 shows a modified Gantt project management organizer for use in upper elementary grade classrooms. You can download this template from the Corwin website by navigating to **www.corwin.com/miningcomplextext/2-5.**

---

1. This section was adapted from a post on LiteracyBeat.com.

FIGURE 9-1
Excel Project Management Organizer

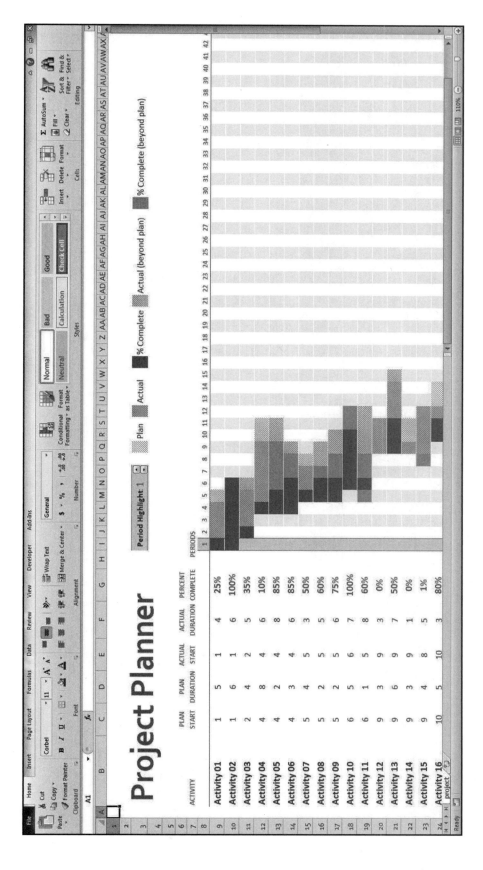

FIGURE 9-2
Smartsheet Project Management Organizer

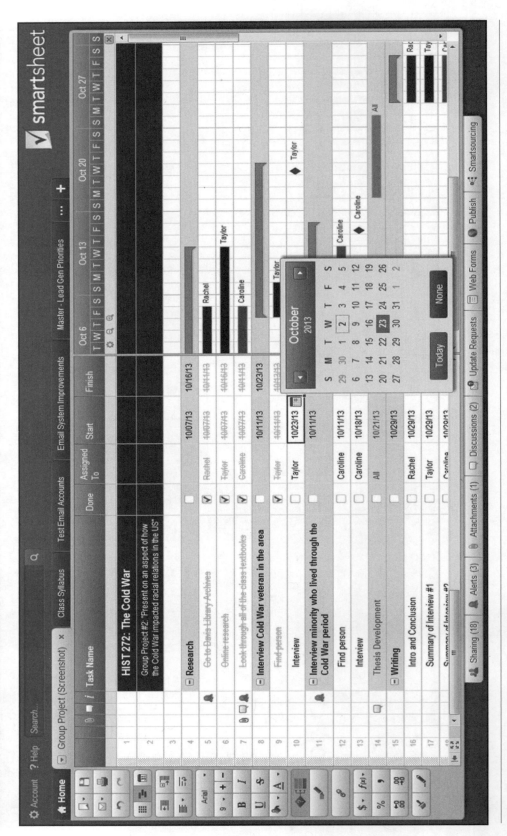

Source: Smartsheet

FIGURE 9-3
Gantt Project Management Organizer

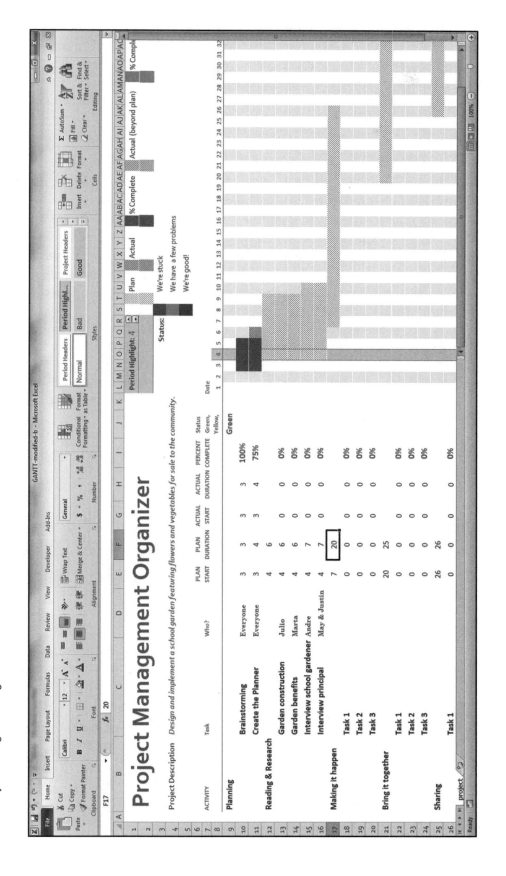

Both of these organizers allow students to quickly enter data about what they plan to do, how much they have accomplished, and how they are proceeding. The neat thing is that Excel and other spreadsheet software automatically create the timeline showing what is planned and what is actually accomplished. These examples show a start date for the first of the month, but teachers can create their own template by deleting columns for dates that don't match the instructional cycle.

How Do I Use a Project Management Organizer?

- As we discussed in Chapter 1, some skill development is necessary with graphic organizers. With project management organizers, students need to know why the tool will help them be successful with the project, what norms (Cohen, 1994) they will need to work in groups, and how to use the technology itself, even if that technology is paper or sticky notes! Share models based on previous small projects using a digital projector or document camera, depending on the format. Demonstrate how changing the values (usually these values are dates) in the plan, actual, and percent columns changes the timeline to the right automatically.

- Train a few students, perhaps one from each project group or team, to be the group expert on using technology. In this way, you are not the only resource for using the tool.

- Help students define the major parts of the task. In the example in Figure 9-3, the teacher defined large categories as *planning, reading and research, making it happen, bringing it together, and sharing.*

- Assist students with breaking down each category into specific tasks. A model will be very helpful in guiding students to decide just what the specific tasks might be.

- Start the project!

INTO THE CLASSROOM

Fifth Grade—Science and Language Arts

THIS CLASSROOM EXAMPLE ADDRESSES THESE STANDARDS

CCSS.ELA-Literacy.SL.5.1.

Engage effectively in a range of collaborative discussions (one-on-one, in groups, and teacher-led) with diverse partners on grade 5 topics and texts, building on others' ideas and expressing their own clearly.

CCSS.ELA-Literacy.SL.5.1a.

Come to discussions prepared, having read or studied required material; explicitly draw on that preparation and other information known about the topic to explore ideas under discussion.

CCSS.ELA-Literacy.SL.5.6.

Adapt speech to a variety of contexts and tasks, using formal English when appropriate to task and situation.

Determining the Need

Mr. Jardiner's students approached science by getting their hands right into the thick of things. They surveyed the area around the school for rock formations, modeled how waves destroy communities during particularly powerful storms, and now, one group was ready to engage in a bit of dirty work. They planned to put their spades right into the soil in a part of the schoolyard to build a garden that would be beautiful but also produce vegetables for the community. They would have to work collaboratively, read many resources, convince others of the project's value, and then make the school garden happen (see Wolsey, 2014).

The students at Tuileries Elementary School were very accustomed to having their voices be part of the school community. The podiums in the auditoriums were not just for the administrators and teachers; they were also for any student who had something to say. The main lobby was a gathering place for students, parents, and teachers where ideas were explored and problems solved (see Uline, Tschannen-Moran, & Wolsey, 2009). They were not surprised when Mr. Jardiner asked them to think of a service learning project that would benefit the community. One group chose to focus on a school garden that would produce vegetables they might sell to the community at cost because so many families had to travel long distances by bus just to purchase fresh produce.

Introducing It

Once students had decided on their projects, Mr. Jardiner demonstrated how students could use Excel to organize the project so that they kept to timelines and succeeded. He chose several students to serve as Excel masters who could help solve problems when they arose, and they were excused from other tasks so they could explore online tutorials and play around a bit with the project management organizer. To make sure students stayed on task, Mr. Jardiner adjusted the template to show the timelines for the project, then placed it on the class web page for students to download.

Guided and Independent Practice

Students worked together to create a plan using the project management organizer and decide just what steps they would need to take. Every 3 days, students met with Mr. Jardiner to show him their organizer and ask questions about the next steps. The school garden group created an organizer, which you can see in Figure 9-3.

Mr. Jardiner inserted the plan dates into the template. He knew that students would need to present this to the school board on the 26th day, and actual timelines based on the board meeting dates would be critical. Students worked through the project, and as they moved from one major category to another, they added the specific steps they would need to take. Maria volunteered to keep the project management organizer updated and posted to the group blog so they could each review it every day.

Closure

At the end of the project, students had designed a garden and obtained the permission of the principal and school board to make it happen. They had also created a schedule for maintaining the garden and invited other students to participate. Before long, the school garden project was selling produce, at cost, to the parents who came to school to pick up children or participate in parent-teacher-student events.

Reading, Writing, and Discussion Extensions

Throughout any project, many opportunities exist for discussion, speech, writing, and reading. Teachers may choose to make these components explicit parts of the project depending on curricular goals. Our objective in including this project management organizer is that it is infinitely adaptable and expandable, and it provides students with a way to organize how they engage in literacy tasks as they collaborate with each other.

CONCLUSION

Throughout this text we have shared many graphic organizers that support students as they read and organize information and also as they organize ideas and information they plan to share through written or oral presentations. As we have emphasized throughout, we encourage you to use these examples to model for students the power of using graphic organizers. But this isn't where we want you to stop. We encourage you to also help students realize that they can construct organizers to promote and share their thinking. It is through their individual construction that they will think deeply about the information they are learning or presenting. This personalization promotes their independence as thinkers.

APPENDIX

GRAPHIC ORGANIZERS AT A GLANCE: MEETING EIGHT ESSENTIAL ACADEMIC SKILLS

In the matrix on pages 126–127, we have identified eight essential skills and aligned them with the graphic organizers in this book. It is important to know that the specific tasks, students' capacities for understanding content and processes, and curricular goals may mean that each graphic organizer should be adapted by students and teachers to meet the instructional goals and standards intended.

	1. Acquire and use academic language appropriately	2. Make connections	3. Comprehend complex processes or events	4. Understand five types of informational text structures
Frayer Organizer	x			
Concept/Definition Map	x			
Word Map	x			
Character Graphic		x		
Freytag's Pyramid		x		
Text Search and Find Board		x		
4-Square With a Diamond		x		x
Modified KWL			x	x
Tabbed Book Manipulative	x	x	x	x
Five Text Types				x
Sequential			x	x
Descriptive				x
Cause/Effect		x		x
Compare and Contrast		x		x
Problem/Solution		x	x	x
I-Chart and I-Guide				
Flip Chart Manipulative				x
Text-Dependent Question/Response Organizer		x	x	x
Six-Part Opinion Organizer				
Thinking Map				
Project Management Organizer		x		

	5. Understand content	6. Explore a concept and determine the nature of inquiry	7. Synthesize multiple sources	8. Use reliable sources to form and write opinions
Frayer Organizer	x			
Concept/Definition Map	x			
Word Map	x			
Character Graphic	x			
Freytag's Pyramid				
Text Search and Find Board	x			
4-Square With a Diamond	x			
Modified KWL	x	x	x	
Tabbed Book Manipulative	x	x		
Five Text Types				
Sequential	x			
Descriptive	x			
Cause/Effect	x			
Compare and Contrast	x			
Problem/Solution	x			
I-Chart and I-Guide		x	x	
Flip Chart Manipulative	x			
Text Dependent Question/ Response Organizer	x			
Six-Part Opinion Organizer	x	x		x
Thinking Map	x	x	x	x
Project Management Organizer		x		

FRAYER ORGANIZER

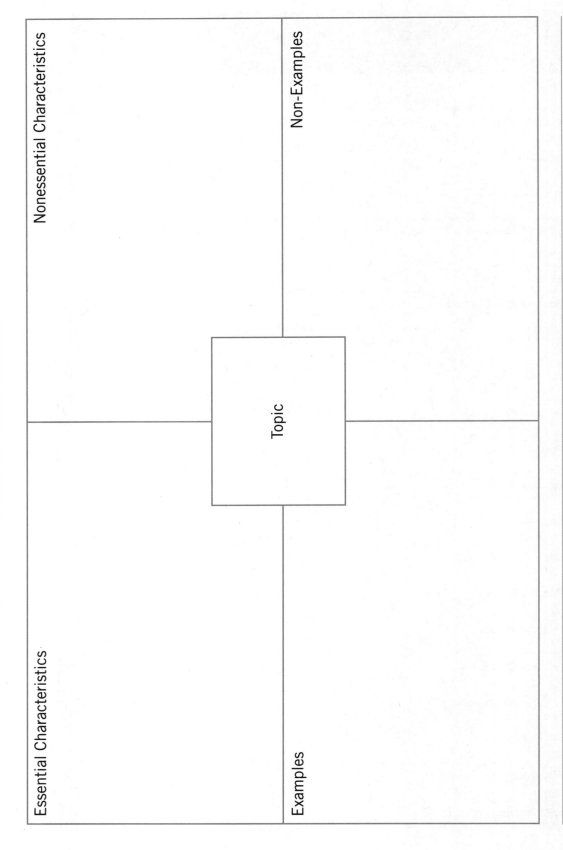

Essential Characteristics

Nonessential Characteristics

Topic

Examples

Non-Examples

Source: Adapted from the original Frayer Model, created by Dorothy Frayer, University of Wisconsin.

Available for download from www.corwin.com/miningcomplextext/2-5

Reprinted from *Mining Complex Text, Grades 2–5: Using and Creating Graphic Organizers to Grasp Content and Share New Understandings* by Diane Lapp, Thomas DeVere Wolsey, and Karen Wood. Thousand Oaks, CA: Corwin, www.corwin.com. Reproduction authorized only for the local school site or nonprofit organization that has purchased this book.

CONCEPT/DEFINITION MAP

Name:

Date:

Subject:
Topic, Word, or Concept:

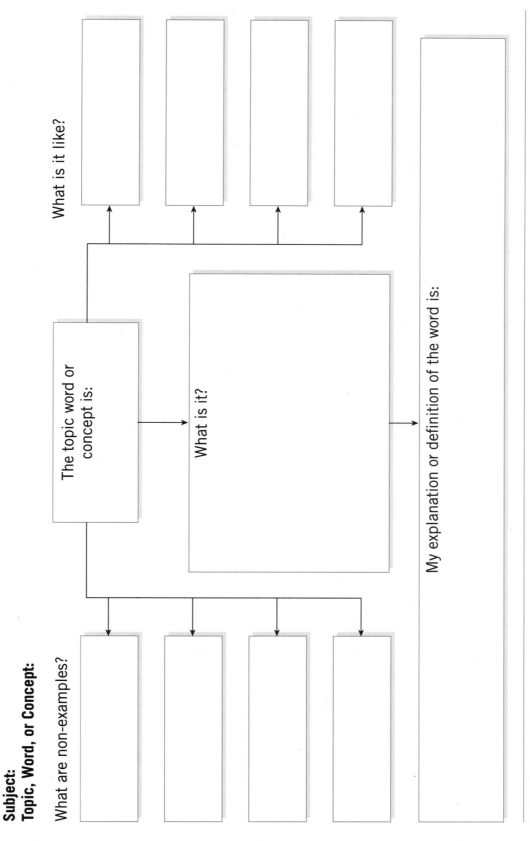

What is it like?

The topic word or concept is:

What is it?

What are non-examples?

My explanation or definition of the word is:

WORD MAP

The word is:

Dictionary definition:

Word used in the sentence from the book or lecture:

Synonyms and related words:

Symbol or picture:

Two examples of how the word can be used in your own life:

Explanation of symbol or picture:

CHARACTER GRAPHIC

Name: _____

Title: _____ **Author:** _____

Character

What does the character look like?

What happened in the story? What might you have done if you were the character?

What things does the character do?

What do you like or dislike about the character? Why?

What is something important to know about this character?

Source: Adapted from *Character Connections,* Florida Center for Reading Research, 2007.

Available for download from **www.corwin.com/miningcomplextext/2-5**

CHARACTER GRAPHIC FOR YOUNGER STUDENTS

Name: _____

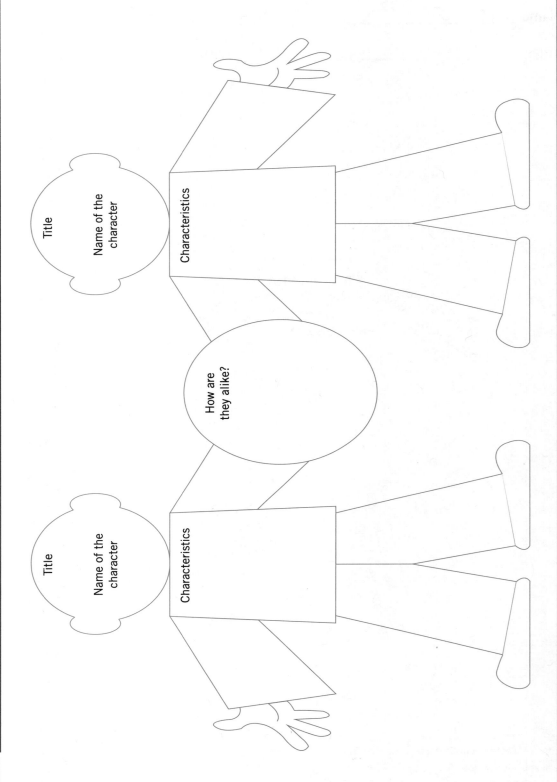

Title

Name of the character

Characteristics

How are they alike?

Title

Name of the character

Characteristics

Source: Adapted from *Character Connections*, Florida Center for Reading Research, 2007.

Available for download from www.corwin.com/miningcomplextext/2-5

Reprinted from *Mining Complex Text, Grades 2–5: Using and Creating Graphic Organizers to Grasp Content and Share New Understandings* by Diane Lapp, Thomas DeVere Wolsey, and Karen Wood. Thousand Oaks, CA: Corwin, www.corwin.com. Reproduction authorized only for the local school site or nonprofit organization that has purchased this book.

CHARACTER GRAPHIC FOR
UPPER ELEMENTARY STUDENTS

Name: _____

_____
_____
_____
_____

How are they alike?

Title: _____

Character #1: _____

Title: _____

Character #2: _____

_____
_____
_____
_____
_____
_____
_____
_____

_____
_____
_____
_____
_____
_____
_____
_____

Source: Adapted from *Character Connections*, Florida Center for Reading Research, 2007.

Available for download from **www.corwin.com/miningcomplextext/2-5**

Reprinted from *Mining Complex Text, Grades 2–5: Using and Creating Graphic Organizers to Grasp Content and Share New Understandings* by Diane Lapp, Thomas DeVere Wolsey, and Karen Wood. Thousand Oaks, CA: Corwin, www.corwin.com.

FREYTAG'S PYRAMID

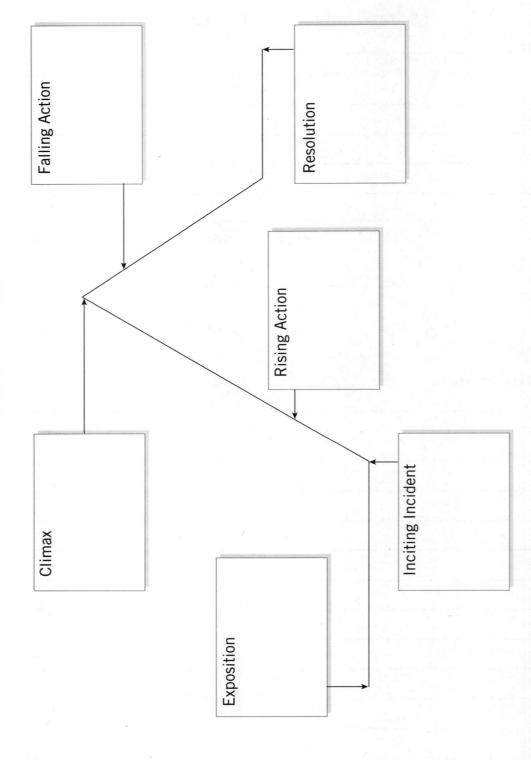

Exposition

Inciting Incident

Rising Action

Climax

Falling Action

Resolution

Source: Adapted from Holman and Harmon, 1992.

Available for download from www.corwin.com/miningcomplextext/2-5

Reprinted from *Mining Complex Text, Grades 2–5: Using and Creating Graphic Organizers to Grasp Content and Share New Understandings* by Diane Lapp, Thomas DeVere Wolsey, and Karen Wood. Thousand Oaks, CA: Corwin, www.corwin.com. Reproduction authorized only for the local school site or nonprofit organization that has purchased this book.

TEXT SEARCH AND FIND BOARD

Title	Main Idea	Key Details	Vocabulary
Include the book title and your name here.	*What's the main idea? Write a complete sentence that tells the main idea.*	*Provide at least three key facts that support your main idea.*	*List and define at least three important vocabulary words from the book.*
Connections *How does this text remind you of something in your life or another text you have read?*	**Chart, Illustration, or Graph** *Create a chart, illustration, or graph to display some of the information you learned from the book.*	**Questions** *After reading your book, create questions.*	**Answers** *Choose at least one of your questions and provide an answer with supporting details from the text.*

Source: Created by Rebecca Kavel.

Available for download from **www.corwin.com/miningcomplextext/2-5**

Reprinted from *Mining Complex Text, Grades 2–5: Using and Creating Graphic Organizers to Grasp Content and Share New Understandings* by Diane Lapp, Thomas DeVere Wolsey, and Karen Wood. Thousand Oaks, CA: Corwin, www.corwin.com.

4-SQUARE WITH A DIAMOND

I know:

Brainstorm: What might work?

I need to know:

Try it:

Explain what you now know.

KWL

K **What do we know about the KWL instructional strategy?**	W **What do we want to know about the KWL instructional strategy?**	L **What did we learn about the KWL instructional strategy?**

Categories:

SOMEBODY-WANTED-BUT-SO

Somebody (Characters)	
Wanted (Plot motivation)	
But (Conflict)	
So (Resolution)	

SEQUENTIAL

- Steps
- Specific order

1.

2.

3.

4.

5.

DESCRIPTIVE

CAUSE/EFFECT

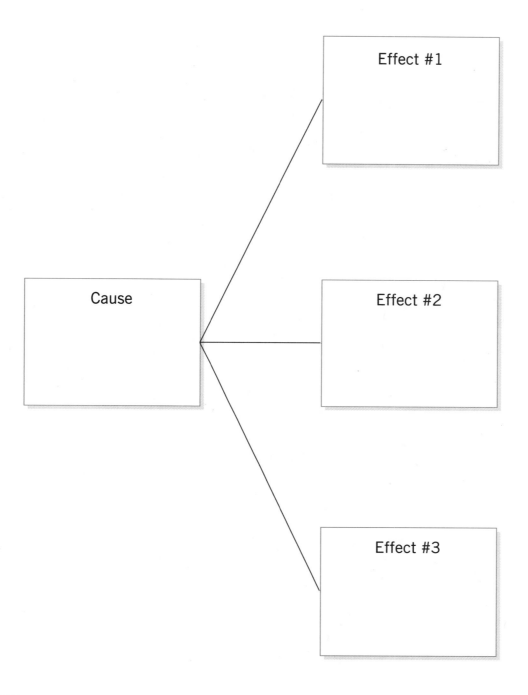

COMPARE AND CONTRAST

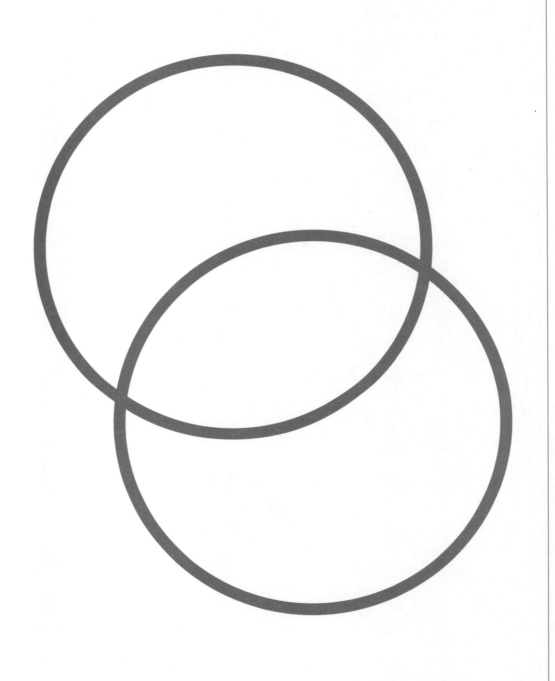

PROBLEM/SOLUTION

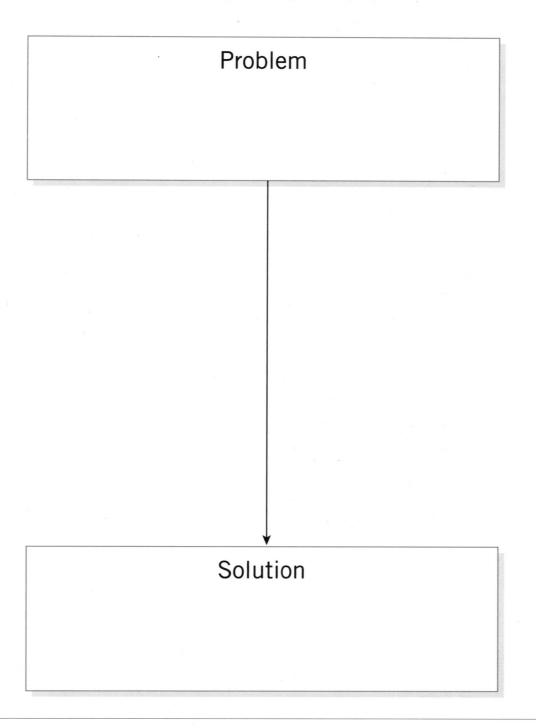

COMPARE-AND-CONTRAST ATTRIBUTE CHART

Name:

Date:

Subjects:

Topic or Concepts:

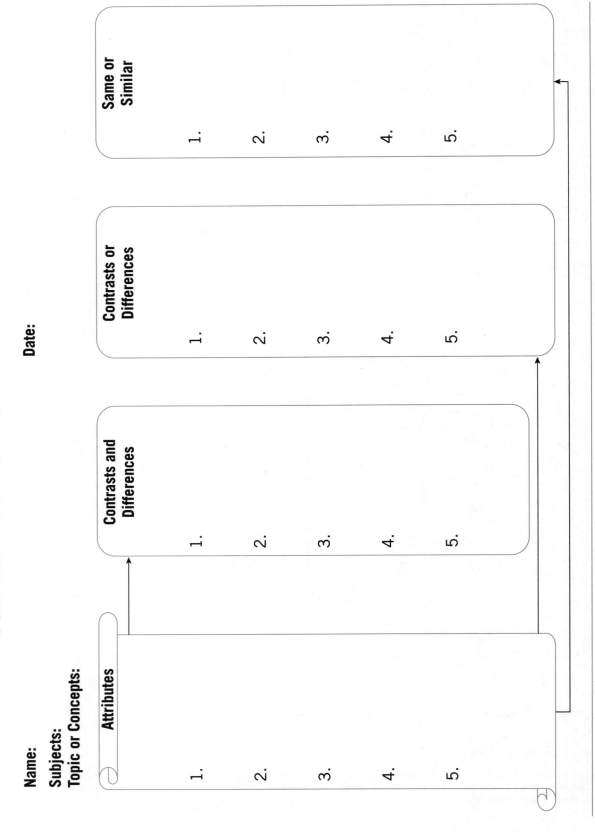

Attributes	Contrasts and Differences	Contrasts or Differences	Same or Similar
1.	1.	1.	1.
2.	2.	2.	2.
3.	3.	3.	3.
4.	4.	4.	4.
5.	5.	5.	5.

PROBLEM/SOLUTION GRAPHIC ORGANIZER

Name:

Date:

Subjects:
Topic or Concepts:

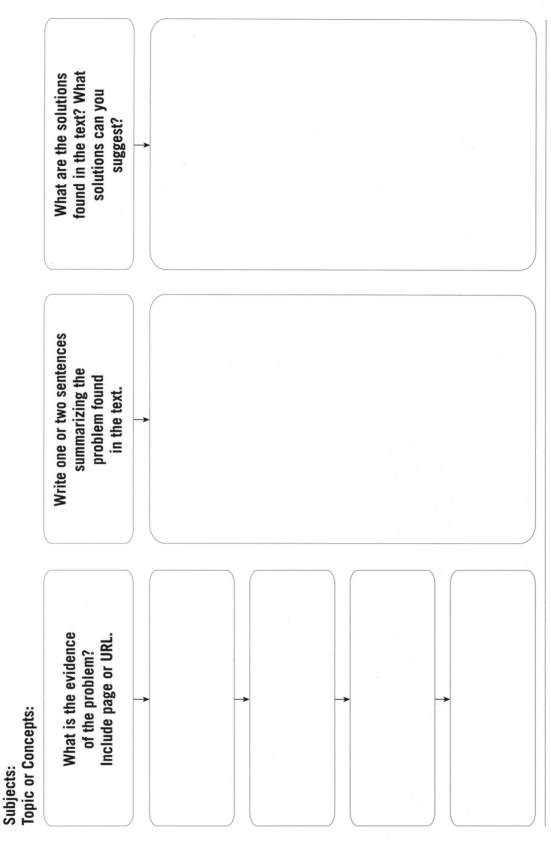

What is the evidence of the problem? Include page or URL.

Write one or two sentences summarizing the problem found in the text.

What are the solutions found in the text? What solutions can you suggest?

I-CHART

What We Know					
Topic	Question	Question	Question	Other Interesting Facts and Figures	New Questions
Sources					
Synthesis					

I-GUIDE

What We Know						
Topic or Question	**Major Subtopics or Themes**		**Summary of Each Text**		**Importance or Relevance of the Information**	
Sources						
Synthesis						

TEXT-DEPENDENT QUESTION/RESPONSE ORGANIZER

Name: _____ Date: _____

Subject: _____

Circle one:

- This is my first reading
- Second reading
- Third or more readings

The text-dependent question is:

After reading the text again, I found this evidence to support my answer (with page numbers):

And now my response to the question is:

SIX-PART OPINION ORGANIZER

Explain an opinion you have about this topic:	
Topic:	
Opinion:	
1. My current position is:	**2. What I think the position of others might be:**
3. The response of others to my opinion could be:	**4. My response to them is:**
5. How do I know?	**6. How has my opinion changed?**

THINKING MAP

Thinking Map: What Do I Know?

Decision 1: Identify your initial knowledge.
- What do I know?
- Are my sources trustworthy?
- Write an outline.

→ Write your brief outline here or on the back of the page.

Decision 2: Read many different sources.
- What comes up often?
- Are there ideas that make a pattern?
- Expand outline.

→ Read many sources until you notice a pattern. Keep notes on a different page and then identify the pattern here.

Decision 3: Self-talk about growing knowledge.
- Vocabulary I need
- What is not clear to me?
- My point of view
- Related topics

→ Notes here.

Decision 4: Has my knowledge or point of view changed?
- What are my reasons?
- How do I know they are good reasons?

→ Notes here.

Decision 5: What new questions do I have? Note them here.

Available for download from www.corwin.com/miningcomplextext/2-5

Reprinted from *Mining Complex Text, Grades 2–5: Using and Creating Graphic Organizers to Grasp Content and Share New Understandings* by Diane Lapp, Thomas DeVere Wolsey, and Karen Wood. Thousand Oaks, CA: Corwin, www.corwin.com. Reproduction authorized only for the local school site or nonprofit organization that has purchased this book.

GLOSSARY

Academic language is characterized by word choice (see academic vocabulary as well as the syntactic structures that make deep connections). It is also a term used to describe the language that students and scholars might employ in their academic work.

Academic vocabulary describes the function of academic vocabulary in terms of complexity, higher-order thinking, and abstraction. The terms associated with these functions are usually thought of as they relate to a specific discipline (e.g., science, social studies) and to those that are typically used in academic environments but are used across disciplines (Coxhead, 2000). Tier two vocabulary (Beck, McKeown, & Kucan, 2002) are those terms that are mainly specific to academic environments but cut across disciplines. Tier three vocabulary, by contrast, are typically specific to a domain. We encourage you to read more about these topics by consulting Coxhead (2000) and Beck et al. (2002).

Advance organizers (Ausubel, 1960) are often thought of as synonymous with graphic organizers; however, the two terms are not interchangeable. Advance organizers are presented, as the name implies, in advance of new concept learning. They are typically graphical in nature, but they need not be. Graphic organizers may be used throughout any learning sequence. A structured overview is a type of graphic organizer that demonstrates connections among broad topics in advance of learning.

Digital environment is a term that describes interactions between humans in an electronic environment.

Gradual release of responsibility implies a method whereby the teacher initially has responsibility for student learning, often through direct instruction (see Durkin, 1990), but students are increasingly given responsibility for understanding the processes, conditions, and tasks of the learning.

Literature circles (Daniels, 2002) are designed to foster a love of reading and for students to "work together to choose literature they wish to read and explore collaboratively" (Wolsey, 2004, para. 1).

Manipulatives (including foldables such as those advanced by Zike, n.d.), for the purposes of this book, generally mean a graphic organizer that is in some way manipulated physically, such as by folding paper, by the student.

Scaffold is a term first conceived by Bruner (1978) to describe the helping interaction found in Vygotsky's (1978) theories of learning. Scaffolding is a technique by which a teacher or capable peer assists a student, often through the use of tools such as a graphic organizer, to make sense of what would otherwise be nearly incomprehensible. The principle of scaffolding rests on the notion that it is only useful if the student cannot proceed efficiently or meaningfully without the assistance. For the purposes of this book, a graphic organizer must promote student learning independently or it would not be considered a scaffold.

REFERENCES

Akhondi, M., Malayeri, F., & Samad, A. (2011). How to teach expository text structure to facilitate reading comprehension. *Reading Teacher, 64*, 368-372. doi:10.1598/RT.64.5.9

Anderson, L. W., & Krathwohl, D. R. (Eds.). (2001). *A taxonomy for learning, teaching, and assessing: A revision of Bloom's taxonomy of educational objectives.* New York, NY: Longman.

Ausubel, D. P. (1960). The use of advance organizers in the learning and retention of meaningful verbal material. *Journal of Educational Psychology, 5*, 267–272. doi:10.1037/h0046669

Beck, I. L., McKeown, M. G., & Kucan, L. (2002). *Bringing words to life: Robust vocabulary instruction.* New York, NY: Guilford Press.

Birbili, M. (2006). Mapping knowledge: Concept maps in early childhood education. *Early Childhood Research and Practice, 8*, 1–11.

Bluestein, N. A. (2013). Comprehension through characterization: Enabling readers to make personal connections with literature. *Reading Teacher, 55*, 431-434.

Braselton, S., & Decker, B. C. (1994). Using graphic organizers to improve the reading of mathematics. *Reading Teacher, 48*, 276–281.

Bruner, J. (1978). The role of dialogue in language acquisition. In A. Sinclair, R. J. Jarvelle, & W. J. M. Levelt (Eds.), *The child's concept of language* (pp. 241–256). New York, NY: Springer-Verlag.

Candler, L. (2012). *Laura Candler's graphic organizers for reading comprehension.* Saint Johnsbury, VT: Compass Brigantine Media.

Clark, W. (1923). *The Gantt chart: A working tool of management.* New York, NY: Ronald Press. Retrieved from https://archive.org/details/ganttchartworkin00claruoft

Clarke, J. (1994). Sequencing graphic organizers to guide historical research. *Social Studies, 85*(2), 70–75.

Cohen, E. G. (1994). *Designing groupwork: Strategies for the heterogeneous classroom* (2nd ed.). New York, NY: Teachers College Press.

Coleman, D., & Pimentel, S. (2012). *Revised publishers' criteria for the Common Core State Standards in English Language Arts and Literacy, Grades 3–12.* Retrieved from http://achievethecore.org/content/upload/3._Publishers_Criteria_for_Literacy_for_Grades_3-12.pdf

Common Core State Standards Initiative. (2010a). Appendix A: Research supporting key elements of the standards. In *Common Core State Standards for English language arts & literacy in history/social studies, science, and technical subjects.* Retrieved from http://www.corestandards.org/assets/Appendix_A.pdf

Common Core State Standards Initiative. (2010b). *Common Core State Standards for English language arts and literacy in history/social studies, science, and technical subjects.* Retrieved from http://www.corestandards.org/assets/CCSSI_ELA%20Standards.pdf

Concept/definition maps to comprehend curriculum content. (2011). *Reading Teacher, 65*, 211–213. doi:10.1002/TRTR.01029

Coxhead, A. (2000). A new academic word list. *TESOL Quarterly, 34*, 213–238. doi:10.2307/3587951

Daines, D. (1986). Are teachers asking higher level questions? *Education, 106*, 368–374.

Daniels, H. (2002). *Literature circles: Voice and choice in book clubs and reading groups* (2nd ed.). York, ME: Stenhouse.

DiCecco, V. M., & Gleason, M. M. (2002). Using graphic organizers to attain relational knowledge from expository text. *Journal of Learning Disabilities, 35*, 306–320. doi:10.1177/00222194020350040201

Dirksen, D. J. (2011). Hitting the reset button: Using formative assessment to guide instruction. *Phi Delta Kappan, 92*(7), 26–31.

Duke, N. K., & Pearson, P. D. (2002). Effective practices for developing reading comprehension. In A. E. Farstrup & S. J. Samuels (Eds.), *What research has to say about reading instruction* (3rd ed., pp. 205–242). Newark, DE: International Reading Association.

Durkin, D. (1990). Dolores Durkin speaks on instruction. *Reading Teacher, 43,* 472–726.

Fisher, D., & Frey, N. (2012a). *Improving adolescent literacy* (3rd ed.). New York, NY: Pearson.

Fisher, D., & Frey, N. (2012b). Text dependent questions. *Principal Leadership, 13*(3), 70–73.

Fisher, D., Frey, N., & Lapp, D. (2012). *Text complexity: Raising rigor in reading.* Newark, DE: International Reading Association.

Florida Center for Reading Research. (n.d.). *Comprehension: Narrative text structure, character consideration.* Retrieved from http://www.fcrr.org/curriculum/PDF/G4-5/45CPartOne.pdf

Gallagher, K. (2011). *Write like this: Teaching real-world writing through modeling and mentor texts.* Portland, ME: Stenhouse.

Gallavan, N. P., & Kottler, E. (2010). Visualizing the life and legacy of Henry VIII: Guiding students with eight types of graphic organizers. *Social Studies, 101,* 93–102. doi:10.1080/00377991003711699

Gardner, H. (2006). *Changing minds: The art and science of changing our own and other people's minds.* Boston, MA: Harvard Business School Press.

Gick, M. L., & Holyoak, K. J. (1983). Schema induction and analogical transfer. *Cognitive Psychology, 15,* 1–38. doi:10.1016/0010-0285(83)90002-6

Gill, S. (2007). Learning about word parts with Kidspiration. *Reading Teacher, 61,* 79–84. doi:10.1598/RT.61.1.8

Gillis, V. (2014). Disciplinary literacy: Adapt not adopt. *Journal of Adolescent and Adult Literacy, 57,* 614–623. doi:10.1002/jaal.301

Griffin, C. C., Malone, L. D., & Kameenui, E. J. (1995). Effects of graphic organizer instruction on fifth-grade. *Journal of Educational Research, 89*(2), 98–107. doi:10.1080/00220671.1995.9941200

Hartman, D. K. (1995). Eight readers reading: The intertextual links of proficient readers reading multiple passages. *Reading Research Quarterly, 30,* 520–561.

Harvey, S., & Goudvis, A. (2000). *Strategies that work: Teaching comprehension to enhance understanding.* Portland, ME: Stenhouse.

Hoffman, J. V. (1992). Critical reading/thinking across the curriculum: Using I-charts to support learning. *Language Arts, 69,* 121–127.

Holman, C. H., & Harmon, W. (1992). *A handbook to literature* (6th ed.). New York, NY: Macmillan.

Hunter, M. (1982). *Mastery teaching.* Thousand Oaks, CA: Corwin.

Hyde, A. (2006). *Comprehending math: Adapting reading strategies to teach mathematics, K–6.* Portsmouth, NH: Heinemann.

IRIS Center. (n.d.). *What should content-area teachers know about vocabulary instruction?* Page 7: Building vocabulary and conceptual knowledge using the Frayer model. Retrieved from http://iris.peabody.vanderbilt.edu/module/sec-rdng/cresource/what-should-content-area-teachers-know-about-vocabulary-instruction/sec_rdng_07

Ives, B. (2007). Graphic organizers applied to secondary algebra instruction for students with learning disorders. *Learning Disabilities Research & Practice, 22,* 110–118. doi:10.1111/j.1540-5826.2007.00235.x

Ives, B. B., & Hoy, C. C. (2003). Graphic organizers applied to higher-level secondary mathematics. *Learning Disabilities Research & Practice, 18,* 36–51. doi:10.1111/1540-5826.00056

Lapp, D., Thayre, M., & Wolsey, T. D. (2014). *Arguments are only as credible as their sources: Teaching students to choose wisely.* Available from http://www.reading.org

Lorenz, B., Green, T., & Brown, A. (2009). Using multimedia graphic organizer software in the pre-writing activities of primary school students: What are the benefits? *Computers in the Schools, 26,* 115–129. doi:10.1080/07380560902906054

Macon, J., Bewell, D., & Vogt, M. (1991). *Responses to literature.* Newark, DE: International Reading Association.

Marzano, R. J., Pickering, D. J., & Pollock, J. E. (2001). *Classroom instruction that works: Research-based strategies for increasing student achievement.* Alexandria, VA: Association for Supervision and Curriculum Development.

McLaughlin, M., & Overturf, B. J. (2013). *The Common Core: Graphic organizers for teaching K–12 students to meet the reading standards.* Newark, DE: International Reading Association.

McMackin, M. C., & Witherell, N. L. (2005). Different routes to the same destination: Drawing conclusions with tiered graphic organizers. *Reading Teacher, 59,* 242–252. doi:10.1598/RT.59.3.4

Meyer, B. J. F., Brandt, D. M., & Bluth, G. J. (1980). Use of top-level structure in text: Key for reading comprehension of ninth-grade students. *Reading Research Quarterly, 16,* 72–103. doi:10.2307/747349

Moje, E. B. (2007). Developing socially just subject-matter instruction: A review of the literature on disciplinary literacy teaching. *Review of Research in Education, 31*, 1–44. doi: 10.3102/0091732X07300046001

Novak, J. D., & Musonda, D. (1991). A twelve-year longitudinal study of science concept learning. *American Educational Research Journal, 28*, 117–153. doi:10.3102/00028312028001117

Ogle, D. (1986). K-W-L: A teaching model that develops active reading of expository text. *Reading Teacher, 39*, 564–570.

Olson, C. B. (1996). Integrating clustering and showing, not telling. In C. B. Olson (Ed.), *Practical ideas for teaching writing as a process at the elementary and middle school* (Rev. ed., pp. 52–54). Sacramento: California Department of Education.

Olson, P. (1968). Introduction: On myth and education. In P. Olson (Ed.), *The uses of myth: Papers relating to the Anglo-American seminar on the teaching of English at Dartmouth College, New Hampshire 1966.* Champaign IL: National Council of Teachers of English.

Raphael, T. E. (1984). Teaching learners about sources of information for answering questions. *Journal of Reading, 27*, 303–311.

Raphael, T. E. (1986). Teaching question-answer relationships, revisited. *Reading Teacher, 39*, 516–520.

Reardon, C., & Vossler, T. (2013). *The Gettysburg campaign, June–July 1863* (CMH Pub 75-10). Washington, DC: U.S. Army, Center of Military History. Retrieved from http://www.history.army.mil/html/books/075/75-10/CMH_Pub_75-10.pdf

Richardson, A. (1983). Imagery: Definitions and types. In A. A. Sheikh (Ed.), *Imagery: Current theory, research, and application* (pp. 3–42). New York, NY: John Wiley & Sons.

Sadoski, M., & Paivio, A. (2004). A dual coding theoretical model of reading. In R. B. Ruddell & N. Unrau (Eds.), *Theoretical models and processes of reading* (5th ed., pp. 1329–1362). Newark, DE: International Reading Association.

Schwartz, R. M., & Raphael, T. E. (1985). Concept of definition: A key to improving students' vocabulary. *Reading Teacher, 39*, 198–205.

Shanahan, T., & Shanahan, C. (2008). Teaching disciplinary literacy to adolescents: Rethinking content-area literacy. *Harvard Educational Review, 78*(1), 40–59.

Sundeen, T. H. (2007). So what's the big idea? Using graphic organizers to guide writing for secondary students with learning and behavioral issues. *Beyond Behavior, 16*(3), 29–34.

Tomlinson, C. A. (1999). *The differentiated classroom: Responding to the needs of all learners.* Upper Saddle River, NJ: Merrill Education.

Townsend, D. R., & Lapp. D. (2010). Academic language, discourse communities, and technology: Building students' linguistic resources. *Teacher Education Quarterly.* Retrieved from http://teqjournal.org/townsend_lapp.html

Uline, C., Tschannen-Moran, M., & Wolsey, T. D. (2009). The walls still speak: A qualitative inquiry into the effects of the built environment on student achievement. *Journal of Educational Administration, 47*, 395–420. doi:10.1108/09578230910955818

Vansledright, B. (2012). Learning with texts in history: Protocols for reading and practical strategies. In T. Jetton & C. Shanahan (Eds.), *Adolescent literacy in the academic disciplines: General principles and practical strategies* (pp. 199–227). New York, NY: Guilford Press.

Vygotsky, L. S. (1978). *The mind in society: The development of higher psychological processes.* Cambridge, MA: Harvard University Press.

Wallace, D. F. (1997). The string theory. In G. Plimpton (Ed.), *1997: The best American sports writing* (pp. 249–282). Boston, MA: Houghton Mifflin.

Wolsey, T. D. (2004). Literature discussion in cyberspace: Young adolescents using threaded discussion groups to talk about books. *Reading Online, 7*(4). Retrieved from http://www.readingonline.org

Wolsey, T. D. (2014). The school walls teach: Student involvement in the green school. In T. C. Chan, E. G. Mense, K. E. Lane, & M. D. Richardson (Eds.), *Marketing the green school: Form, function, and the future.* Hershey, PA: Information Science Reference/IGI.

Wolsey, T. D., Grisham, D. L, & Heibert, E. (2012). *Teacher development series.* Retrieved from http://textproject.org/professional-development/teacher-development-series

Wolsey, T. D., & Lapp, D. (2009). Discussion-based approaches for the secondary classroom. In K. Wood & B. Blanton (Eds.), *Promoting literacy with adolescent learners: Research-based instruction* (pp. 368–391). New York, NY: Guilford Press.

Wolsey, T. D., Lapp, D., & Fisher, D. (2012). Students' and teachers' perceptions: An inquiry into academic writing. *Journal of Adolescent and Adult Literacy, 55*, 714–724. doi:10.1002/JAAL.0086

Wood, K. D. (1998). Guiding readers through informational text. *Reading Teacher, 41*, 912–920.

Wood, K. D., Lapp, D., Flood, J., & Taylor, B. T. (2008). *Guiding readers through text: Strategy guides in "new times."* Newark, DE: International Reading Association.

Zike, D. (n.d.). *Dinah Zike's reading and study skills foldables*. New York, NY: McGraw-Hill Glencoe.

Zollman, A. (2009). Mathematical graphic organizers. *Teaching Children Mathematics, 16,* 222–230.

Zull, J. E. (2002). *The art of changing the brain: Enriching teaching by exploring the biology of learning.* Sterling, VA: Stylus.

Children's Literature Cited:

Alexander, C. L. (2007). *Ghost ship on the cay: A 15-minute ghost story.* Los Gatos, CA: LearningIsland.com. Retrieved from https://www.smashwords.com/books/view/138359

Bradbury, R. (1962). *Something wicked this way comes.* New York, NY: Bantam.

Deluise, D. (1990). *Charlie, the caterpillar.* New York, NY: Aladdin Paperbacks.

Hiaasen, C. (2002). *Hoot.* New York, NY: Alfred A. Knopf.

Hinton, S. E. (1967). *The outsiders.* New York, NY: Dell.

Keady, D. (2012, October 31). Sandy's aftermath. *Time for Kids.* Retrieved from http://www.timeforkids.com/news/sandys-aftermath/57171

McDermott, G. (1972). *Anansi the spider: A tale from the Ashanti.* New York, NY: Henry Holt.

Modigliani, L. (2011, June 13). Sharks in hot water. *Scholastic News Online.* Retrieved from http://www.scholastic.com/browse/article.jsp?id=3756258p?id

Sahagun, L. (2013, May 26). Too few great white sharks? *Los Angeles Times,* A31, A32.

Sharp, T. (2012, November 27). Superstorm Sandy: Facts about the Frankenstorm. *LiveScience.* Retrieved from http://www.livescience.com

Van Allsburg, C. (1986). *The stranger.* Boston, MA: Houghton Mifflin.

Wallace, D. F. (1997). The string theory. In G. Plimpton (ed.), *The best American sports writing, 1997* (pp. 249–282). Boston, MA: Houghton Mifflin.

Warren, S. (2013, September). Washed away. *SuperScience 25*(1), 4–7. Retrieved from http://browndigital.bpc.com/publication/?i=165832

INDEX

Academic goals list
  1: acquire and use academic language appropriately, 8–9
  2: making connections, 9
  3: comprehension of complex processes or events (sequences), 9
  4: understanding five types of informational text structures, 9–10
  5: understand content, 10
  6: explore a concept and determine the nature of inquiry, 10
  7: synthesize multiple sources, 10–11
  8: use reliable sources to form and write opinions, 11
  See also CCSS (Common Core State Standards)
Academic goals
  at-a-glance chart of graphic organizers matched to, 31
  Common Core State Standards to meet eight intertwined, 3 (figure)–11
Academic language skills
  academic goal of acquiring and using, 8–9
  graphic organizers to increase vocabulary, 33–45
  how graphic organizers can help achieve, 9
Academic vocabulary
  concept/definition map for building, 39 (figure)–42 (figure)
  Frayer organizers for building, 34 (figure)–38 (figure)
  word map for building, 43 (figure)–45
Advance organizers, 22
Akhondi, M., 79, 81
Anansi the Spider: A Tale From the Ashanti (McDermott), 85–86
Aristotle, 81
Assessment tools, 24
Ausubel, D. P., 22

Battle of Gettysburg (U.S. Civil War), 16, 17
Beck, I. L., 44
Bewell, D., 74
Birbili, M., 49

Blank graphic organizers, 23
Bluestein, N. A., 49
Bluth, G. J., 79
Bradbury, R., 81
Brandt, D. M., 79
Braselton, S., 22
Brown, A., 89

Candler, L., 58
Cause/effect text structure
  description and applications of, 82
  herringbone or fishbone diagrams visual of, 82
  illustration of, 79 (figure)
CCSS (Common Core State Standards)
  aligning lesson ideas with, 2–3
  description of, 3
  how to meet eight intertwined academic goals of the, 3 (figure)–11
  calling for graphic organizers, 4–7
  See also Academic goals list
CCSS (Common Core State Standards) Initiative, 12, 73
CCSS ELA literacy anchor standards
  character graphic to facilitate learning, 48, 51
  comparing across the grades, 106–108
  concept/definition map to facilitate learning, 39, 41
  description of, 3
  flip chart manipulative to facilitate learning, 97, 98
  4-square with a diamond to facilitate learning, 62, 63
  Frayer organizer to facilitate learning, 34, 35
  Freytag's pyramid to facilitate learning, 53, 54
  I-chart and I-guide to facilitate learning, 92, 94
  modified KWL to facilitate learning, 65, 67
  project management organizer to facilitate learning, 116, 120

somebody-wanted-but-so to facilitate learning, 74, 76

tabbed book manipulative to facilitate learning, 70, 71

text search and find board to facilitate learning, 58, 59

on text structures, 78 (figure), 86, 87

text-dependent question/response to facilitate learning, 99, 101

thinking map to facilitate learning, 111, 113

tiered interactive picture book read aloud to facilitate learning, 27

word map to facilitate learning, 43, 44

Character Connections (Florida Center for Reading Research), 49

Character graphics

CCSS ELA literacy anchor standards facilitated by, 48, 51

description and example of, 48 (figure)–49

example suitable for upper elementary students, 50 (figure)

example suitable for younger students, 49 (figure)

how to use for students, 49, 51

second grade–historical figures, 51–52

Charlie, the Caterpillar (Deluise & Santoro), 76–77 (figure)

Circle map, 26 (figure)

Clark, W., 116

Clarke, J., 26

Classroom examples

fifth grade–ecosystems, 67–69

fifth grade–opinion writing, 109–110

fifth grade–science and language arts, 120–122

fifth grade–U.S. government, 35–37

fourth grade–extreme weather, 94–96

fourth grade–learning to ask and research relevant questions, 113–114

fourth grade–math, 63–64 (figure)

fourth grade–realistic fiction, 54–56

fourth grade–science, 41–42 (figure)

fourth grade–text structure, 87–89

second grade–reading, 98

second grade–retelling/summarizing, 76–77 (figure)

third grade–reading, 71–72 (figure)

third grade–space, 44–45

third/fourth grade–astronomy, 59–61 (figure)

See also Instruction

Cognitive load, 81

Cohen, E. G., 120

Coleman, D., 12

Collaboration

fifth grade–science and language arts classroom on, 120–122

project management organizer for, 116–122

Compare and contrast text structure

description and applications of, 83

illustration of, 79 (figure)

online resource for compare-and-contrast attribute chart, 84–85 (figure)

Venn diagrams graphic organizers for, 83–84 (figure)

Complex text. *See* Reading text

Complexity

academic goal of comprehension of, 9

description of, 9

how graphic organizers can help with, 9

modified levels of complexity or depth organizers, 23

Comprehension. *See* Reading/reading comprehension

Concept/definition maps

CCSS ELA literacy anchor standards facilitated by, 39, 41

description of, 1, 39 (figure)–40

example of students,' 42 (figure)

fourth grade–science classroom example using, 41–42 (figure)

how to use a, 40

originally developed for science instruction, 25

websites that provide an outlet for, 40

Concepts

academic goal of determining nature of inquiry and exploring a, 10

how graphic organizers can help to use in inquiry stance, 10

Connections. *See* Making connections

Content

academic goal of, 10

how graphic organizers can help with understanding, 10

modified for individualized instruction, 24–26 (figure)

summarizing, 71

Content areas

somebody-wanted-but-so example for history, 75–76 (figure)

somebody-wanted-but-so example for math, 75 (figure)

Daines, D., 100

"Decisive Moments in the Battle of Gettysburg" graphic organizer, 17

Decker, B. C., 22

Deluise, D., 76

Descriptive text structure
    description and applications of, 81–82
    illustration of, 79 (figure)
    visual representations of words and ideas
        online, 82 (figure)
DiCecco, V. M., 22
Digital graphic organizers
    "Decisive Moments in the Battle of
        Gettysburg," 17
    Frayer *Republic* example using Prezi
        software, 36 (figure)
    Frayer template using Prezi software,
        37 (figure)
    tips on using, 21
Dirksen, D. J., 24
Disciplinary literacy, 21
Discussion
    fifth grade–ecosystems, 69
    fifth grade–opinion writing, 110
    fifth grade–science and language arts, 121
    fifth grade–U.S. government, 37
    fourth grade–extreme weather, 96
    fourth grade–learning to ask and research
        relevant questions, 114
    fourth grade–math, 64
    fourth grade–realistic fiction, 55
    fourth grade–science, 45
    fourth grade–text structure, 89
    second grade–historical figures, 52
    second grade–reading, 98
    second grade–retelling/summarizing, 77
    third grade–reading, 72
    third grade–space, 45
    third/fourth grade–astronomy, 61
Duke, N. K., 58

ELA (English Language Arts). *See* CCSS ELA
    literacy anchor standards
European Organization for Nuclear Research
    (CERN) website
    graphic organizer to understand
        "matter particles" text on the,
        19–20 (figure)
    standard model of particle physics as
        described on the, 19 (figure)
Excel project management organizers,
    116, 117 (figure)

Farrow, J., 48
Fifth grade
    ecosystem classroom for, 67–69
    inferring while reading classroom for,
        101–103
    opinion writing classroom for,
        109–110
    progression of text structure types in the
        CCSS for, 78 (figure)

science and language arts classroom for,
    120–122
U.S. government classroom for,
    35–38 (figure)
First grade
    CCSS ELA literacy anchor standard
        1 for, 106
    progression of text structure types in the
        CCSS for, 78 (figure)
Fishbone diagram, 82
Fisher, D., 100, 110
Five text structures. *See* Text structures
Flip chart manipulative organizers
    CCSS ELA-literacy anchor standards
        facilitated by, 97, 98
    description and example of, 97 (figure)
    how to use a, 97
    second grade–reading, 98
Flood, J., 70, 92
Florida Center for Reading Research, 49
For Kids search tool, 94
Formative assessment tools, 24
4-square with a diamond organizers
    CCSS ELA literacy anchor standards
        facilitated by, 62
    description and illustration of,
        62 (figure)
    fourth grade–math classroom example
        using, 63–64 (figure)
    how to use a, 63
    rubric for, 64 (figure)
Fourth grade
    astronomy classroom for, 59–61 (figure)
    extreme weather classroom for, 94–96
    learning to ask and research relevant
        questions classroom for, 113–114
    math classroom for, 63–64 (figure)
    progression of text structure types in the
        CCSS for, 78 (figure)
    realistic fiction classroom for, 54–56
    science classroom for, 41–42 (figure)
    text structure classroom for, 87–89
Frayer, D., 34
Frayer organizers
    CCSS ELA-literacy anchor standards
        facilitated by, 34, 35
    digital *Republic* example using Prezi
        software, 36 (figure)
    digital template using Prezi software,
        37 (figure)
    handwritten Frayer for *accelerate* from
        science reading, 38 (figure)
    how to use a, 34–35, 38
    illustration adopted from original Frayer
        Model, 34 (figure)
Frey, N., 100
Freytag, G., 53

Freytag's pyramids
    CCSS ELA literacy anchor standards
        facilitated by use of, 53
    description and illustration of, 53 (figure)
    fourth grade–realistic fiction classroom
        example using, 54–56
    how to use a, 53–54
    website resource on, 54

Gallagher, K., 109
Gallavan, N. P., 80
Gantt, H., 116
Gantt project management organizers,
    116, 119 (figure)
Gardner, H., 10
Gettysburg, battle of (U.S. Civil War),
    16, 17
Ghost Ship on the Cay: A 15-Minute Ghost Story
    (Alexander), 102
Gick, M. L., 83
Gill, S., 40
Gleason, M. M., 22
Goodard, R., 44
Google Drive, 44
Goudvis, A., 9
Grade K CCSS ELA literacy anchor standard
    1, 106
Grade 1
    CCSS ELA literacy anchor standard
        1 for, 106
    progression of text structure types in
        the CCSS for, 78 (figure)
Grade 2
    CCSS ELA literacy anchor standard 1
        for, 106
    flip chart manipulative organizer for
        reading for, 98
    historical figures classroom for, 51–52
    progression of text structure types in the
        CCSS for, 78 (figure)
    summarizing/retelling classroom for,
        76–77 (figure)
Grade 3
    astronomy classroom for, 59–61 (figure)
    CCSS ELA literacy anchor standard 1 for,
        106–107
    progression of text structure types in the
        CCSS for, 78 (figure)
    space classroom for, 44–45
Grade 4
    astronomy classroom for, 59–61 (figure)
    CCSS ELA literacy anchor standard
        1 for, 107
    extreme weather classroom for, 94–96
    learning to ask and research relevant
        questions classroom for, 113–114
    math classroom for, 63–64 (figure)

progression of text structure types in the
    CCSS for, 78 (figure)
realistic fiction classroom for, 54–56
science classroom for, 41–42 (figure)
text structure classroom for, 87–89
Grade 5
    CCSS ELA literacy anchor standard
        1 for, 107
    ecosystem classroom for, 67–69
    inferring while reading classroom for,
        101–103
    opinion writing classroom for, 109–110
    progression of text structure types in the
        CCSS for, 78 (figure)
    science and language arts classroom for,
        120–122
    U.S. government classroom for,
        35–38 (figure)
Grade 6 CCSS ELA literacy anchor
    standard 1, 108
Graphic organizer types
    advance, 22
    blank, 23
    interactive, 16–17, 27–30 (figure)
    modified levels of complexity or depth, 23
    partially filled-out, 22
    tiered, 22–30 (figure)
    See also Student-created or -modified
        organizers
Graphic organizers
    adapting for tiered learning, 26–27
    concept/definition maps,
        1, 25, 39 (figure)–42 (figure)
    description and function of, 1
    examining the questions on how to best
        use, 1–2
    increasing academic vocabulary using,
        33–45
    matching academic goals to, 31
    nonlinguistic representation versus, 17
    research on how they work, 15–18
    selected anchor standards calling for use
        of, 4–7
    structured overview of this book on, 14
    when not to use, 23
    See also specific organizers
Graphic organizers tips
    be explicit, 18
    on dynamic use of graphic organizers, 7–8
    to differentiate instruction, 20
    to focus on key attributes and concepts, 18
    to help "slice the surface" of a text,
        19 (figure)–20 (figure)
    to help students learn in each
        discipline, 21
    for use as digital or hard-copy
        handouts, 21

Green, T., 89
Griffin, C. C., 22
Grisham, D. L., 73
Guided and independent practice
  fifth grade–ecosystems, 68
  fifth grade–inferring while reading, 102
  fifth grade–opinion writing, 110
  fifth grade–science and language arts, 121
  fifth grade–U.S. government classroom,
    36–37
  fourth grade–extreme weather, 95
  fourth grade–learning to ask and research
    relevant questions, 113–114
  fourth grade–math, 63
  fourth grade–realistic fiction, 55
  fourth grade–science classroom, 41
  fourth grade–text structure, 88
  second grade–historical figures, 52
  second grade–reading, 98
  second grade–retelling/summarizing, 76
  third grade–reading, 72
  third grade–space, 45
  third/fourth grade–astronomy, 60

Harahus, J., 62
Hard-copy vs. digital graphic organizers, 21
Harmon, W., 53
Harry Potter series, 75, 83
Harry Potter and the Sorcerer's Stone
    (Rowling), 75
Hartman, D. K., 9
Harvey, S., 9
Heibert, E., 73
Herringbone diagram, 82
Hiaasen, C., 54
Hinton, S. E., 84
History lessons
  fifth grade–U.S. government,
    35–38 (figure)
  graphic organizers used in, 25–26 (figure)
  Modified KWL organizer example for,
    66 (figure)
  somebody-wanted-but-so organizer
    example for, 75–76 (figure)
  timelines used in, 80–81
Hoffman, J. V., 92
Holman, C. H., 53
Holyoak, K. J., 83
Hoot (Hiaasen), 54–55
Hoy, C. C., 80
Hyde, A., 65

I-charts
  CCSS ELA-literacy anchor standards
    facilitated by, 92, 94
  fourth grade–extreme weather classroom
    on using, 94–96

how to use a, 92, 94
illustration of a, 93 (figure)
KWL format parallels with, 92
I-guides
  CCSS ELA-literacy anchor standards
    facilitated by, 92, 94
  fourth grade–extreme weather classroom
    on using, 94–96
  how to use a, 92, 94
  illustration of a, 93 (figure)
  KWL format parallels with, 92
Ideas
  Freytag's pyramid to identify text,
    53 (figure)–56
  organizers to promote independent
    thinking and use of, 23
  summarizing text, 71, 76–77 (figure)
  tiered organizers to scaffold student
    progress of identifying, 22–23
  visual representations of descriptive text
    structure and, 82 (figure)
  See also Reading/reading comprehension
Independent thinking, 23
Individualized instruction, 24
Inferring
  fifth grade–inferring while reading,
    101–103
  text-dependent question/response
    organizers used for, 100–101
Informational text reading/writing tasks
  4-square with a diamond to support, 62
    (figure)–64 (figure)
  modified KWL to support, 65 (figure)–69
  tabbed book manipulative to support, 70
    (figure)–72 (figure)
  text search and find board to support,
    58 (figure)–61
Informational text structures
  academic goal of understanding five
    types of, 9
  how graphic organizers help with
    understanding, 9–10
Inquiry
  academic goal of determining nature
    of, 10
  definition of, 92
  graphic organizers used in stance
    of, 10
  I-charts and I-guides used for, 92–96
  synthesizing multiple sources during
    process of, 10–11
  using reliable sources to form and write
    opinions during, 11
Instruction
  graphic organizers to differentiate, 20
  graphic organizers to modify content for
    differentiated, 24–26 (figure)

scaffolding, 20, 22–24, 100–101
See also Classroom examples; Lessons;
    Scaffolding
Interactive graphic organizers
    "Decisive Moments in the Battle of
        Gettysburg," 17
    making connections through the use
        of, 16–17
Interactive picture book read-aloud lesson,
    27–30 (figure)
ipl2's For Kids search tool, 94
Ives, B. B., 80

Kameenui, E. J., 22
Kavel, R., 58
Kids.gov, 113
Kindergarten CCSS ELA literacy anchor
    standard 1, 106
Knowledge maps, 1
Kottler, E., 80
Kucan, L., 44

Language anchor standards. *See* CCSS ELA
    literacy anchor standards
Lapp, D., 9, 22, 70, 92, 100, 110
Learning
    graphic organizers for specific discipline, 21
    graphic organizers to differentiate
        instruction for, 20
    how visuals quicken text, 17–18,
        26 (figure), 82 (figure)
    tiered organizers used for, 22–30 (figure)
Lessons
    reading, 54–56, 71–72 (figure),
        98, 101–103
    social studies and history, 25–26 (figure),
        35–38 (figure), 66 (figure),
        75–76 (figure), 80–81
    See also Instruction; Science lessons
Listening anchor standards. *See* CCSS ELA
    literacy anchor standards
Literary text reading/writing tasks. *See*
    Reading text tasks; Writing tasks
Lorenz, B., 89

McDermott, G., 85
McKeown, M. G., 44
McLaughlin, M., 22
McMackin, M. C., 22, 27
Macon, J., 74
Making connections
    the academic goal of, 9
    blank graphic organizers used for, 23
    how graphic organizers facilitate,
        9, 16–17
    interactive graphic organizers used for,
        16–17

reading about U.S. Civil War battle at
    Gettysburg and, 16, 17
types of tiered graphic organizers used for,
    22–23
Malayeri, F., 79
Malone, L. D., 22
Marzano, R. J., 71
Math lessons
    fourth grade–math, 63–64 (figure)
    math flip chart used for, 97 (figure)
    processes or procedures used in, 80
    somebody-wanted-but-so example for,
        75 (figure)
"Matter particles" paragraph,
    19–20 (figure)
Merritt, L., 36, 37, 43
Meyer, B. J. F., 79
Miller, S., 84
Mind maps, 1
Modeling reading, 102
Modified KWL organizers
    CCSS ELA literacy anchor standards
        facilitated by use of, 65, 67
    description and examples of,
        65 (figure)–66 (figure)
    fifth grade–ecosystems classroom example
        using, 67–69
    how to use a, 66–67
    parallels between I-charts and I-guides
        and, 92
Modified levels of complexity or depth
    organizers, 23
Modigliani, L., 67
Moje, E. B., 21
Musonda, D., 25

New York Times, 83
Nonlinguistic representation, 17
Novak, J. D., 25

Ogle, D., 65, 92
Olson, C. B., 82
Olson, P., 55
Online resources. *See* Website resources
"Operation Woodpecker" (*Ranger Rick*
    magazine), 87–88
Opinion writing
    academic goal of using reliable
        sources for, 11
    CCSS ELA literacy anchor standard 1
        across the grades, 106–108
    fifth grade–opinion writing classroom,
        109–110
    how graphic organizers can help during
        formation of, 11
    six-part opinion organizer for,
        108 (figure)–109

The Outsiders (Hinton), 84 (figure)
Overturf, B. J., 22

padlet.com, 40
Paivio, A., 17
Partial herringbone timeline, 26 (figure)
Partially filled-out organizers, 22
Pearson, P. D., 58
Pickering, D. J., 71
Pimentel, S., 12
Pollock, J. E., 71
PowerPoint, 44
Practice. *See* Guided and independent
    practice
Prezi software
    adapting word maps using, 44
    digital Frayer *Republic* example using,
        36 (figure)
    digital Frayer template using, 37 (figure)
prezi.com, 40
Problem/solution text structure
    Anansi the Spider: A Tale From the Ashanti
        used to explore, 85–86 (figure)
    description and applications of, 85
    illustration of, 79 (figure)
Processing, 80
Project management organizers
    CCSS ELA literacy anchor standards
        facilitated by, 116, 120
    description of, 116–120
    Excel, 116, 117 (figure)
    fifth grade–science and language arts
        classroom for, 120–122
    Gantt, 116, 119 (figure)
    how to use a, 120
    Smartsheet, 116, 118 (figure)

Ramadan, K. H., 70, 72
Ranger Rick magazine, 87
Raphael, T. E., 39, 100
Reading assignments
    fifth grade–ecosystems, 69
    fifth grade–inferring while reading, 103
    fifth grade–opinion writing, 110
    fifth grade–science and language arts, 121
    fifth grade–U.S. government classroom, 37
    fourth grade–extreme weather, 96
    fourth grade–learning to ask and research
        relevant questions, 114
    fourth grade–math classroom, 64
    fourth grade–realistic fiction, 55
    fourth grade–science, 42
    fourth grade–text structure, 89
    second grade–historical figures, 52
    second grade–reading, 98
    second grade–retelling/summarizing, 77
    third grade–reading, 72

third grade–space, 45
third/fourth grade–astronomy, 61
Reading lessons
    fifth grade–inferring while reading,
        101–103
    fourth grade–realistic fiction, 54–56
    second grade–reading, 98
    third grade–reading, 71–72 (figure)
Reading/reading comprehension
    character graphic used to support literary,
        48 (figure)–53
    of complex processes or events, 3, 9
    Freytag's pyramid used to support literary,
        53 (figure)–56
    general tips on effective graphic organizer
        use for, 18–21
    graphic organizers to help "slice the
        surface" for, 19 (figure)–20 (figure)
    graphic organizers to promote independent
        thinking and, 23
    inferring role in, 100–103
    making connections role in, 9, 16–17,
        22–23
    modeling, 102
    summarizing for, 71, 76–77 (figure)
    of text content, 10
    thinking map for, 111–114
    visuals to facilitate, 17–18, 25 (figure)–26
        (figure), 82 (figure)
    See also Ideas; Text tasks
Reardon, C., 16
Retelling/summarizing
    description and function of, 71
    second grade–retelling/summarizing
        classroom on, 76–77 (figure)
Richardson, A., 17
Rocket Man (Goddard), 44–45
Rowling, J. K., 75, 83

Sadoski, M., 17
Sahagun, L., 67
Samad, A., 79
San Francisco Chronicle, 83
Scaffolding
    graphic organizers to differentiate
        instruction, 20
    text-dependent question/response
        organizers used for, 100–101
    tiered organizers used for, 22–24
    See also Instruction
Scholastic (magazine), 67
Schwartz, R. M., 39
Science lessons
    fifth grade–ecosystems, 67–69
    fifth grade–science and language arts,
        120–122
    fourth grade–extreme weather, 94–96

fourth grade–science, 41–42 (figure)
fourth grade–text structure, 87–89
modified KWL example for, 66 (figure)
tabbed book manipulative example for, 70 (figure)
third grade–space, 44–45
third/fourth grade–astronomy, 59–61 (figure)
water cycle, 25 (figure)–26 (figure)
See also Lessons
Second grade
flip chart manipulative organizer for reading for, 98
historical figures classroom for, 51–52
progression of text structure types in the CCSS for, 78 (figure)
summarizing/retelling classroom for, 76–77 (figure)
Sequential text structure
description of, 80
illustration of, 79 (figure)
processing, 80
timelines, 80–81
Shanahan, C., 21, 66
Shanahan, T., 21, 66
Six-part opinion organizer, 108 (figure)–109
"Slice the surface," 19 (figure)–20 (figure)
Smartsheet project management organizers, 116, 118 (figure)
Social studies lessons
fifth grade–U.S. government, 35–38 (figure)
graphic organizers used in, 25–26 (figure)
Modified KWL organizer example for, 66 (figure)
somebody-wanted-but-so organizer example for history, 75–76 (figure)
timelines used in history, 80–81
Somebody-wanted-but-so organizers
CCSS ELA literacy anchor standards facilitated by, 74, 76
content area examples of using, 75 (figure)–76 (figure)
description and illustration of, 74 (figure)
for *Harry Potter and the Sorcerer's Stone*, 75 (figure)
how to use the, 74–75
second grade–retelling/summarizing classroom, 76–77 (figure)
Something Wicked This Way Comes (Bradbury), 81
standard model of particle physics, 19 (figure)–20
The Stranger (Van Allsburg), 27
Student-created or -modified organizers
description of, 23
4-square with a diamond, 64 (figure)

Freytag's pyramid, 56
I-guide on erosion, 96 (figure)
modified KWL, 268 (figure)
second grade–retelling/summarizing, 77
tabbed book manipulative, 72 (figure)
text search and find board, 61 (figure)
See also Graphic organizer types
Students
tiered organizers to scaffold progress times, 22–24
when not to use graphic organizers, 23
Summarizing/retelling
description and function of, 71
second grade–retelling/summarizing classroom on, 76–77 (figure)
Sundeen, T. H., 89
SuperScience magazine, 94
Synthesizing multiple sources
academic goal of, 10–11
how graphic organizers can help for, 11

Tabbed book manipulative organizers
CCSS ELA literacy anchor standards facilitated by use of, 70, 71
description and examples of, 70 (figure)
how to help students create a, 70–71
summarizing for, 71
third grade–reading classroom use of, 71–72 (figure)
Taylor, B. T., 70, 92
Teachers
graphic organizers used for formative assessment by, 24
tips on effective use of graphic organizers for learning, 18–21
Templates
Frayer organizer using Prezi software, 37 (figure)
Gantt project management organizer, 116
Text search and find board organizers
CCSS ELA literacy anchor standards facilitated by, 48
description and example of, 58 (figure)
how to use a, 59
third/fourth grade–astronomy classroom use of, 59–61 (figure)
Text structures
cause/effect, 79 (figure), 82
CCSS ELA-literacy anchor standards on, 78 (figure), 86, 87
compare and contrast, 79 (figure), 83–85 (figure)
descriptive, 79 (figure), 81–82 (figure)
fourth grade–text structure classroom on, 87–89
how to use them as graphic organizers, 86–87

problem/solution, 79 (figure), 85–86 (figure)

sequential, 79 (figure), 80–81

Text tasks

academic goal of comprehending complex, 9

CCSS anchor standards on reading and comprehension of complex, 3

character graphic to support literary, 48 (figure)–52

4-square with a diamond to support informational, 62 (figure)–64 (figure)

Freytag's pyramid to support literary, 53 (figure)–56

modified KWL to support informational, 65 (figure)–69

tabbed book manipulative to support, 70 (figure)–72 (figure)

text search and find board to support, 58 (figure)–61

See also Reading/reading comprehension

Text-dependent question/response organizers

CCSS ELA-literacy anchor standards facilitated by, 99, 101

description of, 99–101

fifth grade–inferring while reading, 101–103

how to use a, 101

illustration of, 99 (figure)

scaffolding using, 100–101

Thinking maps

CCSS ELA literacy anchor standards facilitated by, 111, 113

description and illustration of a, 111 (figure)–112

fourth grade–learning to ask and research relevant questions classroom use of, 113–114

how to use a, 112

Third grade

astronomy classroom for, 59–61 (figure)

progression of text structure types in the CCSS for, 78 (figure)

space classroom for, 44–45

Tiered learning

adapting graphic organizers for, 26–27

interactive picture book read-aloud lesson for, 27–28

introductory-level graphic for making inferences, 28 (figure)–30 (figure)

Tiered organizers

adapted for tiered learning, 26–27

examples of, 24–26 (figure)

as formative assessment tools, 24

scaffolding student progress times using, 22–24

Timelines

project management organizers, 120

sequential text structure, 80–81

Tomlinson, C. A., 24

Townsend, D. R., 9

U.S. Army, 16

U.S. Civil War battle at Gettysburg, 16, 17

Van Allsburg, C., 27

Vansledright, B., 66

Venn diagrams

description and function of, 83–84

for The Outsiders (Hinton), 84 (figure)

Visuals

circle map, 26 (figure)

deepening text learning through, 17–18

nonlinguistic representation, 17

partial herringbone timeline, 26 (figure)

visual representations of descriptive text structure, 82 (figure)

water cycle, 25 (figure)–26 (figure)

Vocabulary. See Academic vocabulary

Vogt, M., 74

Vossler, T., 16

Wallace, D. F., 81

Water cycle visual, 25 (figure)–26 (figure)

Website resources

compare-and-contrast attribute chart, 84–85 (figure)

concept/definition maps, 40

fifth grade–ecosystems classroom video instructions, 68

Freytag's pyramid, 54

Gantt project management organizer template, 116

graphic organizer on "matter particles" text, 19–20 (figure)

ipl2's For Kids search tool, 94

Smartsheet project management organizers, 116

Venn diagrams, 83

Websites

Corwin, 116

European Organization for Nuclear Research (CERN), 19–20 (figure)

Kids.gov, 113

padlet.com, 40

prezi.com, 40

Williams, B., 74

Witherell, N. L., 22, 27

Wolsey, T. D., 22, 73, 110, 121

Wood, K. D., 70, 92, 97

Word maps
    description of, 43 (figure)–44
    how to use a, 44
    third grade–space classroom example
        using, 44–45
Writing assignments
    fifth grade–ecosystems, 69
    fifth grade–inferring while reading, 103
    fifth grade–opinion writing, 110
    fifth grade–science and language arts, 121
    fifth grade–U.S. government, 37
    fourth grade–extreme weather, 96
    fourth grade–learning to ask and research
        relevant questions, 114
    fourth grade–math, 64
    fourth grade–realistic fiction, 55
    fourth grade–science classroom, 42
    fourth grade–text structure, 89
    second grade–historical figures, 52
    second grade–reading, 98
    second grade–retelling/summarizing, 77
    third grade–reading, 72

third grade–space, 45
third/fourth grade–astronomy, 61
Writing tasks
    anchor standards calling for graphic
        organizers used for, 4–5
    character graphic used to support literary,
        48 (figure)–53
    4-square with a diamond to support
        informational, 62 (figure)–64 (figure)
    Freytag's pyramid used to support literary,
        53 (figure)–56
    modified KWL to support informational,
        65 (figure)–69
    opinion writing, 11, 106–110
    tabbed book manipulative to support
        informational, 70 (figure)–72 (figure)
    text search and find board to support
        informational, 58 (figure)–61

Zike, D., 70
Zollman, A., 62
Zull, J. E., 9

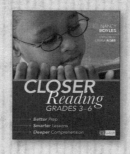

CORWIN
A SAGE Company

Corwin is committed to improving education for all learners by publishing books and other professional development resources for those serving the field of PreK–12 education. By providing practical, hands-on materials, Corwin continues to carry out the promise of its motto: **"Helping Educators Do Their Work Better."**